SUCCESSFULLY SELLING FRANCHISES

JO MIDDLETON

Print ISBN: 978-1-3999-6407-4

eBook ISBN: 978-1-3999-6408-1

Be a good girl.
Be quiet.
Don’t answer back.
Do as you’re told.

What nonsense!

Push the boundaries.
Step into your light.
Question things.
Be hungry to learn more.

You have the power to leave a legacy.

You CAN make your dreams a reality.

Make your own path.

You are enough.

FOREWORD

I am so excited that you have picked up this book. You really do not know what you've got in store. In this book you will learn how to generate an abundance of franchise leads, turn your existing franchisees into lead generating magnets, and grow your franchise network beyond your wildest dreams.

When Jo asked me to write the foreword for her book, I was taken aback and very honoured, because I have always looked up to Jo as an inspiration in the franchising space. She is so knowledgeable and courageous when it comes to growing and scaling not one, but several franchises, and then of course going on to build the franchise business school and support others on their voyage into franchising.

I first came across Jo when we were both nominated for the same award at a very prestigious franchising award ceremony. Jo won and I didn't, and I would be lying if I didn't say a streak of envy ran through me, which I think is natural at these sorts of events. But it did get me thinking, who is Jo Middleton? What is Dog First Aid? And why has she won this award over me? Of course, as soon as I got talking to Jo, I found out she was so kind and genuine and had built a really successful business because she had located a gap in the market, and founded the first ever Dog First Aid franchise. From then on, Jo and I have become good friends. We've worked together, we've recommended each other and we've learnt from each other and will continue to do so.

Franchising is something I could speak about for hours. It's such a great way of growing and scaling a business while giving others the opportunity to have a piece of the pie and grow their own business with your blueprint. I have worked with a number of franchisees over the years. Once they've franchised their business, that's when the hard work begins. Selling your first franchises and then continuing to recruit more and more franchisees is where the real work is. This book is going to be your bible in the franchise recruitment process, which was also my favourite part of my own franchise journey.

Back in 2015, I knew nothing about franchising, or this whole world. My sister, Alex Burnside, and I had founded a company called Phonics with Robot Reg which had gone from strength to strength as an independent children's activities business. So much so that people had started reaching out to us and asking if there were any franchises available. We were flattered, but politely said no, we were just two mums running classes around our young kids. But it planted an idea in our minds which we just couldn't seem to shake off. Did we have something franchisable? Were we sitting on more opportunities than we realised? And the answer was yes. Yes, we were.

We franchised the business and 12 months later we started with three pilot franchisees. Fast forward 18 months and we had sold 30 franchises,

I was head of sales (which later became my biggest passion, which is why I run the business I do now) so my biggest accolade was when we sold that thirtieth franchise the month I turned 30 years old. The newspapers picked up the story and ran with it. '30 franchises before 30' was all over the headlines, and we were so proud of all that we had achieved. Now we have 54 franchisees internationally.

Reading that back, I have made it sound like it was simple – all sunshine and rainbows – but that was not the case. Growing and scaling a successful franchise is one of the hardest things to do in business. I remember being absolutely thrilled that we had managed to secure three pilot franchisees, and once they were trained up we were thinking, what's next? Well, we have to get some more, and before we knew it, we were on the hamster wheel of selling franchises.

I have always been passionate about sales. I started my first business when I was 21 and I have successfully scaled three businesses from the ground up. I recognised really early on that sales were the driving force behind any business, and without sales you don't have a business. Finding a sales strategy that works in order to make more franchise sales is key, and then it's a case of rinsing and repeating until you've grown your franchise network to what you want it to be. I meet lots of franchisors who are yet to sell their first franchise, and until you've sold a franchise you are just in fact an independent business owner with an agreement. But the great thing is, it's easy to turn it around. You've done the hard work creating the product, building a business and getting it ready to franchise. As I always claim, 'sales is easy,' you've just got to know what you're doing.

I'm guessing you've picked up this book because you want to recruit more franchisees, and you are definitely in safe hands because Jo certainly knows how to do that. Not only will she show you how to do it ethically, she will make sure that you are finding the right franchisees for your network. This book is going to aid you in finding a sales strategy that works for you and that you feel comfortable with. And I promise you, when you have that, your business will soar. You will also be able to support your franchisees in their sales too so they become fully booked, which will in turn get you more visibility and bring you more franchise leads. When you focus on your sales, good things come your way.

Good luck! I am excited for the growth you are about to have.

Charlie Day

Charlie Day Sales

INTRODUCTION

I am so chuffed that you are holding my book! In fact, I'm still pinching myself that it is actually out there in print and in your hands (or Kindle).

I have jam-packed it with practical steps, resources and exercises to complete. The chapters are deliberately bite-sized, so you can easily reference the sections you need at any one time, and pick it up and put it down as and when you want.

In the world of business, few paths offer the potential for success quite like franchising. It's a journey that can turn a small, local business into a nationwide or even global brand relatively quickly.

It's a journey that can absolutely transform not only your business but also your life.

This comprehensive guide to successfully selling franchises will show you how to unlock the extraordinary potential that is out there for those passionate and driven franchisors who throw themselves whole heartedly in to their franchise success.

Whether you're an aspiring franchisor just turning your business concept into a franchise and recruiting your pilot franchisees, or an established franchisor looking to further evolve and hone your franchise sales strategy, this book is your roadmap to success. If you've ever dreamt of making a lasting impact on your industry, building financial security, and achieving a level of success that can truly change your life, then this book is for you.

For the new franchisor just about to recruit pilot franchisees, Secrets of Successfully Selling Franchises will provide you with the knowledge, tools, and strategies needed to confidently take that first step. It will help you understand exactly how to pave a path forward to achieve your long term goals and the each and every step you need to take to get there.

For the seasoned franchisor, this book offers a fresh perspective on how to leverage your established success and take your franchise to the next level. It will reveal the transformative power of connecting franchise sales strategy with sales mindset providing a holistic approach which allows you to scale your franchise in ways you might never have imagined.

It is no secret how much I love the franchise industry. Taking the decision to expand your business through franchising is not one that is or should be taken lightly. However, when done ethically, franchising can have an amazingly positive ripple effect on everyone involved, not least the end user.

The way I see it, franchising is about transformation. It's about taking a vision, a business model, and a dream, and turning it into a reality that can change lives. Successful franchising has the power to transform not only the lives of the franchisees who become business owners but also your life as the franchisor. It's a journey of growth, achievement, and fulfilment.

I'm going to walk you through the strategies, insights, and real-world examples that will guide you on developing an effect franchisee sales and recruitment process that will last you for years. You'll learn how to create a franchise system that thrives, how to attract the right franchisees, and how to build a brand that stands the test of time. This book will empower you to make informed decisions, avoid common pitfalls, and chart a course toward a future that is not only financially rewarding but also personally fulfilling.

I guess that it would be helpful to let you know a bit about me and how I found my own secret recipes for selling franchises successfully. My journey to this point has been a rollercoaster – I'm not your conventional kinda gal!

WHERE IT ALL BEGAN

I was born in 1977 in a small town in Wiltshire. My dad was a sergeant major and my Belgian mum an A Level language teacher. Eight years later, my little brother appeared (delivered by the stork of course), my dad came out of the army having done his full service, and we moved down to Bournemouth.

I always felt different as a child, like I didn't quite fit in. I'm not sure whether this was because I moved schools many times and perhaps had a touch of imposter syndrome, or because I was brought up bilingual speaking french at home and english at school. Perhaps it was because I was mad about dogs. I spent many a weekend attending shows and completing my junior handling qualifications, knew every dog breed off by heart and spent several evenings a week at dog training clubs.

Despite feeling different, from an early age I had a 'sky's the limit' kind of attitude. I clearly remember creating a school newsletter in my bedroom with a production line and 'employing' my friend to staple all the copies together so we could sell them on the playground.

I've often wondered if entrepreneurialism can be inherited. What do you think? A few years ago, I found out that my great uncle founded one of Belgium's biggest chocolate operations. I had no clue. The merchandise still sells well on eBay which astounds my mum because she recalls playing with it when she was little.

Anyway, the school newsletter didn't make me my millions, much to my dismay, but it was my first stab at business.

MY FIRST REAL SALES EXPERIENCE

After leaving school with 6 GCSEs grade C and above (or Grade 4 and above if you're far more youthful than me), I went on to study Business, Law, Political and Economic Affairs and French at A level. I worked various jobs through my teens, my first doing telesales for a double glazing firm at the age of 15. We were taught to sell hard and the rejection rate was high, as you can imagine. It was my first experience of sales funnels, lead generation and sales incentives. At the same time, I worked as a care assistant in a rest home. Then I taught myself silver service with the help of some family friends who were in the catering industry so that I could waitress at a higher hourly rate. I also did some bar work in local clubs alongside these. Eventually, I ended up working full time in the Post Office. I wanted more though. I knew that one day I wanted to settle down and have a family so I wanted to live my life to the full while I had no ties.

At the grand age of 19, my idea of living life to its fullest was getting a job at Butlins, a British holiday camp. I had a couple of fabulous summers. I fell in love, got my heart broken and made some life-long friends who have been absolute rocks over the years. We partied, we did silly things, and we made memories that still make me smile today.

At the end of a season, I enrolled in a course called Foreign Language for Industry and Commerce (FLIC) at Bournemouth and Poole College of Further Education, and obtained distinction.

I moved to Birmingham soon after gaining my FLIC qualification to be with my then boyfriend. We'd only been together a few months and it became apparent quite quickly after moving up what a sheltered life I'd led up to that point. There was extreme poverty in the area we lived in and crime rates were far higher than anywhere I'd lived before.

SELLING AGAIN AND AGAIN

Soon after moving, I was lucky enough to be offered a place on a language programme in Paris so I moved there for a few months and worked in a tourism office selling attraction tickets for attractions like the Eiffel Tower and Moulin Rouge. The tourism industry was very competitive. Lots of different agencies sold tickets to the same attractions. Salespeople had to be good or they wouldn't sell and therefore receive their commission. I observed the top sellers and practised their mannerisms, mirroring customer hand movements and expressions, and using key phrases. As I observed, it became clear that selling was a process. The seller needs to inject personality and show genuine interest before they try to sell. When the customer had already purchased or developed trust, it was easier to upsell further products or services to them. It worked time and time again. Plus, because I was (and still am) naturally a people pleaser I enjoyed getting to know what people wanted so that I could sell them the right things.

Ever the romantic, I eventually returned to my boyfriend in Birmingham. Before I knew it, I found myself in a very controlling and abusive relationship with him, cut off from my friends and family. It wasn't until I was out of it that I realised just how horrific it actually was. Despite the situation in my personal life I got a job as a bilingual sales and marketing administrator for a number plate company. However, when I was pregnant with my first daughter I was made redundant with no redundancy entitlement. I was flat broke, to the point I used to walk an hour and a half round trip to sneak into the local swimming pool and attend aqua natal classes because I couldn't afford the fuel to drive there, nor the couple of quid it would cost for entry.

I contacted the local Chamber of Commerce and Industry and attended a course about setting up business. It was while working with a business mentor there and gaining support from the fabulous Prince's Trust that I was able to launch my first business, Word Perfect, in 2000. I ran the business until 2004 when I sought paid employment. At this point, my second daughter was around 18 months old and I realised I needed to get a mortgage in an attempt to leave my relationship.

SELF-DEVELOPMENT JOURNEY AND MORE BUSINESSES

In 2007, I found a book in the library called *Change Your Life in Seven Days* by Paul McKenna. I read the book in seven days and it did what it said on the tin. I fled the Midlands with the help of the police and social services to relocate in a different part of the country for both mine and my children's safety. I still have PTSD but that's a whole different story that deserves a book of its own.

We were homeless for some months, crashing on a friend's couch. It was a crazy time. Finally, I was able to rent somewhere, but after just three months the landlords said they were selling the house. I secured a full-time job at the council as the Resources Coordinator setting up an in-house employment agency. It was a diverse and challenging role that taught me a lot about procurement, recruitment, contracts and much more. This employment meant I was able to get a mortgage again and buy a house that the girls and I could call home for the next ten years.

The problem was, I didn't want to be dropping them off at the childminders at the crack of dawn and picking them up after they'd had their tea. I wanted to be the one dropping them to school, picking them up and being there for them in school holidays. So, I retrained as a dog behaviourist and set up a dog behaviour and pet care business. I got a personal credit card and invested in a van. I became friends with another local lady in a similar line of work and we set up puppy classes together. This was my first experience of a business partnership and I learnt a lot. We did everything on the basis of trust and put nothing in writing. There was no exit strategy in mind either.

It was 2010, and I had just over £100 left on my credit card balance when I saw a 30 day business coaching course advertised for £97. I went for it. As a single mum of two with only my unreliable self-employed income paying for the house, some may have called me reckless. It was certainly a risk maxing out my credit card like that. However, that course impacted my business in a fabulous way and I still work with the same coach today (along with many others I've found since then).

I quickly scaled my pet care business until I had a fleet of vans, a team of staff and a pet care manager. My previous training with the Chamber of Commerce and Industry, and the Princes Trust, my business history and all the sales and marketing experience I'd gained over the years, combined with my more recently gained recruitment knowledge stood me in really good stead.

Growing the pet care business into such a large operation also meant that I could give back. When I lived in the Midlands, I rescued a dog and my eyes were opened to the dog welfare challenges in the U.K. Having the flexibility of the pet care business meant that I was able to start fostering rescue dogs. Since then, I have fostered hundreds of dogs that needed help. I stopped counting in 2013 when we got to foster dog number 100. I was also able to volunteer with a local dog rescue centre and provide post-homing behavioural support, help microchip dogs coming in and assess the dogs in kennels.

WHEN MY FRANCHISING JOURNEY STARTED

Around this time, I took one of my own dogs, Flash Gordon, for a walk and he came back to me covered in blood. Although I had done human first aid courses over the years, in the heat of the moment I couldn't translate my skills to help Flash. I didn't apply pressure to the wound, nor did I assess him for a foreign object. I picked him up, ran to the car feeling very light headed and sped to the vets without even calling ahead to make sure there was a vet available.

Luckily, although he had a very serious wound and needed weeks of recovery and some costly vet visits, Flash was okay. But, it had me thinking. I looked around for a course in dog first aid but had to make a three-hour round trip to the nearest, and it didn't fill me with the confidence to act that I wanted. So, I worked with veterinary professionals for months and months putting together a dog first aid course for local pet professionals.

It was early 2013 when I delivered the first course. I sold out quickly, so I had to book a second date to accommodate more people. I posted about it on my pet care business page and was subsequently hired to deliver training for a rescue centre in South Wales. Then I received feedback from an attendee of the very first course. Her dog Lancelot had severed major arteries on some glass out on a walk. The vet said if she hadn't applied the training I'd given her he would have died. This fired me up to sell more and more places on my courses. In a very short period of time, I was suddenly travelling all around the country delivering courses, and taking on a fabulous veterinary nurse to provide some of the training.

What started as me becoming self-employed to spend more time with the girls suddenly meant that I was dragging them around the country, often against their will. That said, my girls are two of the most independent, forward thinking and inspirational people I know. They were answering the phones for the pet care business by the time they were eight years old, setting up stands and selling dog first aid kits by the age of ten, and their customer service skills are next level. I am incredibly proud of them both.

Unfortunately, I encountered some copyright issues with the course materials. I was hired by a celebrity dog trainer to deliver dog first aid training to their clients. I was quite star-struck and even asked for autographs. I feel silly about that now. People arrived in their droves – significantly more than the 30 I had capped the course at so as to ensure a productive learning environment. The first two rows were filled with the dog trainer's employees. A couple of weeks after the course, the dog trainer launched their own dog first aid courses with one of the employees who'd been sat in the front row. I sought legal advice and business advice, and both suggested franchising my dog first aid courses to scale the business, protect it, and allow me to get my work/life balance back. I had considered franchising the pet care business but never dog first aid. No one had ever done it before, so surely it wasn't possible.

Never one to shy away from a challenge, I decided to give it my best shot. Just imagine how many more dogs' lives could be saved if I could set up a franchise!

I became a sponge for all things franchising and burnt the midnight oil reading and researching. Thousands of pounds, many mistakes, a whole heap of hard work and frustration later, I was ready to sell my first pilot territory.

I sold my half of the puppy class business to my business partner, sold the pet care business to one of my employees and decided to solely focus on the franchise.

All my sales and marketing experience once again stood me in good stead. I had been selling from the age of 15 so selling franchise territories felt like a natural progression. It didn't make sense to me to spend thousands more paying someone else to do the franchisee recruitment and generate leads. Why would I rely solely on a third party to grow my franchise network and pay them thousands of my much-needed profit margin? It was far more logical to hone a robust in-house franchise sales system that meant I was able to generate quality leads and recruit more franchisees that were in line with my bigger picture vision for the business.

My fabulous PA was soon super busy, and I needed a VA for my PA! So, I set up a virtual assistant business in 2018 called Purple Frogs which serviced local businesses as well as my own. This was so successful and the general manager loved it so much she bought it from me 18 months later.

When I sold Dog First Aid in 2020 I had a network of franchisees spanning from the north of Scotland down to the Isle of Wight. I learnt some hard lessons along the way, and boy, was it a rollercoaster, but it enabled me to achieve some great things. I won Encouraging Women into Franchising New Woman Franchisor of the Year 2018, Best Franchise Support at the Approved

Franchise Association Awards and had the business named alongside big franchise brands like McDonalds and Subway in the Elite Franchise Top 100 UK Franchises.

While I was selling Dog First Aid, I set up Franchise Business School which I continue to run today. My mission through Franchise Business School is to make franchising easier and more accessible for female business owners. I want to help women implement their own robust internal franchisee sales system so they can attract more leads, increase their sales and grow their network in line with their goals. Through Franchise Business School I have helped over 100 franchisors to recruit more franchisees using my systems.

But now, here they are, laid bare in this book, just for you.

I have put everything into this. Not just a small part of my system, not just the little bit you might need right now. My whole secret recipe that I have spent years tweaking and honing, that has worked for brands in a variety of industries from pet products and services to children's entertainment, is now all yours to implement successfully in your own franchise.

THE FOUNDATIONS

1
FUTURE-PROOFING YOUR FRANCHISE BRAND

Sometimes, as a franchisor, it can feel as though we would lay our life down for our brand. We need to protect it seemingly at all costs, and of course, protect the investment franchisees have made coming on board under the brand's umbrella. We are determined to ensure as far as we possibly can, that we are future proofing the business. But to see the ripple effect of goodness our businesses make on such a larger scale makes it all worthwhile.

Considering what the franchise will look like in ten, 20 or even 50 years' time, can help us to build a robust head office franchise business model as franchisors. Take a moment to picture how you will feel and how the other people in your business will feel, what the business will look like in the future, and how you can start paving the way to that end destination.

You will build your business more purposefully with grit and determination, and you'll be able to reassure franchisees and prospective franchisees that there is longevity, that they have an asset in running a franchise business with you. Not only will this boost the appeal of your brand to prospects, but it will also mean you have a point in the future to grow towards. You wouldn't jump in the car without having a destination in mind. Let's apply the same principle to running a franchise business.

Right now, you may be thinking, "But, Jo I'm not going to be around in 50 years' time," or "I don't want to be a franchisor even ten years down the line". That's okay! By doing this exercise, you'll be building your Head Office business as an asset too. It means you can map out the bigger picture for your brand and define your exit strategy from it too. Anyone looking to buy the business from you will be able to buy in to your end goals for the company, and know the foundations have been firmly laid. They can put their own stamp and twist on them.

In the 2002 research paper "The Effect of Goal Setting on Goal Attainment: A Meta-Analysis of Experimental Studies" by Edwin A. Locke and Gary P. Latham, a meta-analysis of various experimental studies on goal setting is conducted. They found that individuals who set specific and challenging goals and wrote them down were more likely to achieve those goals compared to those who did not write them down. This practice of writing down goals increased commitment, motivation, and focus, ultimately lead to improved goal attainment. We can surmise therefore that if you simply write down your franchise business goals, you are setting your brand up with a hugely increased success rate in achieving them, compared to competing franchises. It gives you a strong market advantage. And, all you are doing is writing out all the stuff that's already in your head about the direction you see your brand going in.

Another technique you can apply here – and have a little fun with – is to use your senses and the power of your subconscious mind. Using as many senses as you can in your goal-setting reinforces the messages that are sent to your brain. Visuals have a link with your subconscious, for example. It aligns your Reticular Activating System (RAS) to look for what you want. Perhaps you're a fan of the Law of Attraction or believe that "thoughts become things". If so, you're right. You are programming your brain to achieve your goals by adding in visuals.

Have you ever noticed if you get a new car, you suddenly see loads of others of the same make and model? Or if you are pregnant, you suddenly see lots of other pregnant people? It's because your RAS is programmed to look for that specific thing.

It's the same with your franchise brand's business vision. If you can become clear on what that vision looks like and feels like to you, and you can associate that vision with the emotions it will inspire when it becomes a reality, you will be able to articulate your mission more clearly to others, and your RAS will naturally programme you to spot opportunities that will take you closer to that vision.

The RAS is described by Allan and Barbara Pease

in their book "The Answer" as follows:

"The RAS is a place where your thoughts, internal feelings and outside influences meet. [...] It is a network of nerve pathways that filter all the sensory input your brain receives from your external world.

Whatever you see, hear, feel or taste passes through the RAS. Put simply, the RAS is the answer to switching on your brain and is the brain's main centre of motivation."

They go on to say, ""The brain processes over 400 million bits of information every second but only 2,000 bits can be processed consciously. [...] In other words, 99.9999 per cent of the information presented to you every day goes unnoticed. This is the only way we can deal with everyday life and the millions of bits of information flooding into our awareness and demanding our attention.

Your RAS functions like a sorting office, evaluating the incoming information and prioritising that information in the form of messages that need your attention. It's a filter between your conscious and subconscious mind, and it takes instructions from your conscious mind and passes them on to your subconscious. Your brain then instructs your body to make the physical actions necessary to comply with the image the RAS instructs. It sorts through your environment for information patterns that best match your beliefs or the things that are familiar to you. Then it links your thoughts and feelings with similar things in your environment. When it finds a match, your conscious mind is alerted."

Start by gathering visual prompts such as images of your dream home, holidays or car for example and place them in areas you spend the most time, so you will see them regularly keeping these hoped for successes present in your mind. For example, if your goal is to have 100 franchisees, or that your network will help 10,000 customers by a particular date, write that number in colourful pen on a Post It note and pop it in the cupboard where you keep your tea bags, so every time you make a cup of tea you are reminded – even if subconsciously – about your goal.

If you have worked on your organisation's vision, mission and values in the past, now is the time to revisit and update them. Revising these ideas and keeping them fresh will lay a firmer foundation for prospective franchisees to buy into your brand.

Franchisees look for certain things when buying into a brand. They may speak to one franchisor who knows what their business will look like ten years down the line, and another who doesn't have the same level of depth and clarity in their corporate vision. Which franchisor are they more likely to buy into? They are unlikely to see the former option as a safe investment as the franchisor don't know themselves what they want to achieve, whereas the latter will inspire confidence as a result of having a vision.

EXERCISE 1

Where will your business BE in ten years?
What does your business need to DO to reach that destination?
What does your franchise need to HAVE now in order to get there?

2
MESSAGING

YOUR EXTERNAL MESSAGING is anything that the public sees, from the look and feel of your offering, your brand and marketing materials, your social media copy, the back links you feature on other sites (e.g. blogs, directories). All of this needs to be on point with the bigger picture vision we worked on in Exercise 1.

QUICK TIPS:

- Short, concise sentences in your messaging will help your audience to quickly digest the information you want them to. The human brain now has a shorter attention span than a goldfish

and it can take 5-27 views of a message before action is taken.
- Provide lots of space between your messaging and make your copy and imagery "scroll stopping". The majority of digital users now access information via their mobile devices. This means that yours needs to stand out from the crowd to stop them scrolling.
- Any more tips? E.g. think about the needs your offering fulfils and highlight those so it resonates with your target customer
- Consider your brand personality, how your brand stands out from competitors. Utilise the brand tone of voice
- Clear calls to action etc.

While I was born and raised in the U.K., I am from a mixed nationality background and I've spent much of my childhood and indeed some of my working career in Europe. It is noticeable to me that the British are perhaps at a disadvantage in the way we greet and converse with others. We tend to be more 'polite' in our brand messaging and include too many instances of, "Please could you xxx", "I would be delighted if you could xxx",

"Thank you so much for xxxx". It may feel overbearing or 'salesy' to use strong calls to action but these actually help our prospective franchisees to discover more about an opportunity that could potentially transform their lives.

Studying the franchise messaging used in other countries like the U.S.A., Canada and Australia can help to open up your thinking about how you craft your own messaging differently and perhaps more progressively. Check out what is happening in your industry in other countries and study different copy and imagery. See what catches your eye and look at how it engages target customers recording growth in direct relation to specific promotions, comments on social media etc to monitor success.

Being clear and direct in your franchise brand messaging, clearly stating statistics and testimonials along with a pointed call to action, will makes it easier for your target customer to take action.

By using my 4 P's system in the next chapter, you will be able to create a clear brand transformation statement that will help you hone your messaging. You will be able to clearly articulate what being a franchisee with your brand could look like. Are your franchisees able to enjoy a better work/life balance where they feel less stressed and more in control of their time and finances? Perhaps they are able to be there to pick their children up for school and take time off in the school holidays as they please, to enjoy making memories with their families?

Top Tip: Write your copy and leave it. Read it a few hours later, or the next day, and try to look at it more from an editorial perspective rather than a heart and head perspective. Try asking yourself these questions: Is it clear what I am offering? Is any information missing? Can I use fewer words?

3
THE 4 P'S OF THE IDEAL FRANCHISEE

JOANNE BUDDEN, owner of Leapfrog Sports, found her biggest learning was that the actual franchising part, preparing the Operations Manual and legal documents, while intense, is only a small part of franchising. "The hardest part is finding the right franchisees. You need to have an audience and know exactly who you are looking for and where to find them, and be clear on how they get to hear about you and how can you stand out to them."

I am making the assumption that by coming as far as franchising your business, you have done some work around ideal customer profiling. This means that your franchisees have clarity on who they are marketing to because they know exactly who they want to attract as customers.

Most franchisors have done ideal franchisee profiling, however, I often find that it isn't being refreshed. Your ideal franchisee profile will change over the course of running your franchise business. You may discover that the original profile you had attracted enquiries from prospective franchisees who were not in line with your brand's bigger picture. Perhaps you have people enquiring about becoming a franchisee who are not able to afford the initial franchise fee or don't understand what a franchise business model is. By changing it up every year and re-evaluating your ideal franchisee profile(s) you can ensure you are attracting the right people.

I go as far as naming my ideal franchisee profiles and give them personalities because it helps me to think of them as humans. It means I can speak to them directly in my messaging.

My ideal franchisee profile for Wizziwoos Kids Clubs is someone who is quite similar to me. They probably love curry and dogs, and enjoy having a work/life balance, being outdoors and splashing in puddles.

I am a big believer in keeping things simple and my 4 P's system is designed to do just that. I brain dump around the 4 P's, research where I can find these types of people and then create a focus group of people who meet that description to pick their brains.

THE 4 P'S

- **Personality:** What are they like? Outgoing or introverted? Bubbly or reserved? Studious? Caring?
- **Profession**: What are they doing now to pay the bills? Did they train to do that? Where did they train? Why are they looking to leave their profession? How do they feel about it now? How did they feel when they were training for it?
- **Pastimes**: Do they like playing golf? Do they go horse riding? Perhaps they enjoy socialising and going out for meals? Maybe they love holidays?
- **Passion**: This one is key but often overlooked. What are they passionate about? Do they support any charitable organisations? Do they raise awareness

for any causes that they feel strongly about?

These pillars will help you to understand your ideal franchisees, and the more work you can do to develop your understanding, the better. Use different colours while you are mind mapping each one. If you can't think of more points, change pen colour to keep the creative juices flowing. If you haven't used this method before, it's a cool visual method for sorting and linking ideas around a central concept. You jot down keywords, draw branches create a non-linear representation of your thoughts.

It is a common mistake to not profile the prospective franchisee that you think will buy in to your brand. This is not how ideal franchisee profiling should be done.

To attract the best fit franchisees to your business, who will pioneer and champion the brand, you need to work on profiling the franchisee that you want to buy in to the brand. The franchisees that will take ownership for their decisions, take business growth actions, maximise the resources you provide them with and comply with the operations manual fully. You want to attract franchisees that take accountability for their businesses and responsibility for the results they generate. You do not want franchisees who engage in any blame games or are in denial about their obligations under the franchise agreement.

Once you know exactly who your ideal franchisees are you can create a clear brand transformation statement which speaks directly to them. For example, Wizziwoos Kids Clubs helps primary school teachers go from feeling burnt out and frazzled to running a fun and rewarding business unlocking the full potential in every child.

It is really powerful to be able to clearly describe the transformation that a franchisee could have by coming on board with your brand. It aids them to visualising what their lives could be like, but also helps with your positive mindset around the value your franchise offering has.

When I franchised a business for the first time I wasn't aware of how widely impactful being a franchisor could be. With Dog First Aid, I had only thought about the impact we would have on the end users. My view was the more franchisees I could onboard successfully, the more dogs lives could ultimately be saved. It wasn't until one of my franchisees explained things from her perspective that I had this massive lightbulb moment. She had trained for many years to become a vet. The amount of work, time and emotional commitment required was extensive. Vet work involves long hours (between 60 and 80 a week) and intense pressure. Becoming a vet was a choice she had made because she loved animals. In reality, she found it to be heart breaking work that was incredibly stressful and had a massive impact on her mental health. Veterinary practice has a scarily high suicide rate. In fact *The Guardian* reported in an article in June 2022 that nearly 70% of veterinarians lost a colleague or peer to suicide.

By buying in to the franchise and running her own business delivering dog first aid training, she was able to have the flexibility and work/life balance she wanted while still helping animals and using her qualifications.

To give someone the opportunity to go from not having control over their lives, to being able to run their own business doing something they love, with all the tools and ongoing support they need to be successful is huge.

A common misconception is that franchisors are alienating other potential franchisees by only marketing to the *ideal* franchisee profile(s). That's not the case. Other enquiries will still come in. You are simply taking a more strategic, targeted approach to your franchisee recruitment to attract those that you want to onboard more quickly and effectively.

Sandra Milena Jurasz-Cruz, owner of El Recreo Spanish Limited, says what worked for her was to choose someone she knew really well for her pilot franchise: "My advice is to be very specific about the person you want to take on board as part of your family, because this is a commitment for years. Get to know this person in a close way if you can. My pilot franchisee is a friend I met at secondary school. We have lot in common, and we have had a very positive experience so far. I think, when recruiting, we need to know as much as we can about someone before making the decision."

EXERCISE 2

Profile your ideal franchisees using the 4 P's and prepare a brand transformation statement to use in your marketing.

4
FRANCHISE SOCIAL PROOF

RUNNING a franchise is a different business to the one that you originally franchised. The ideal franchisee profile you have built is likely to be a different profile to that of the end user of the product or service that your brand provides.

Being a franchisor is a unique position to be in. You have to wear two hats when it comes to your marketing, with one eye on building the brand and attracting end user customers, and the other attracting your ideal franchisees. Having franchise social proof that attracts your ideal franchisees is key to the growth of your network.

So what is franchise social proof? It is the 'band wagon' effect. A psychological phenomenon that persuades the prospective franchisee that there is a lower risk of coming on board because others are doing so successfully. In Robert Cialdini's book, *Influence*, he details the definition of social proof as, "We view a behaviour as more correct in a given situation to the degree that we see others performing it". If you see others doing something, whether it be friends, family or people you've never even met, you are likely to believe what they are doing is good and right.

The six different types of social proof that are particularly relevant in our franchise businesses are:

- **User social proof** – reviews, recommendations, testimonials, public shout-outs from existing franchisees
- **Expert social proof** – association with a thought leader in your industry. You might invite them to take over your social media accounts for a day, or conduct a live interview together that is broadcast on your digital platforms. This provides expert social proof by associating the expert with your brand.

- **Celebrity social proof** – getting a mention on social media from a high profile celebrity adds a layer of social proof. For example, one of the brands I worked for was mentioned on social media by celebrity influencer Mrs. Hynch. This resulted in an influx of online traffic that crashed their website.
- **Friends social proof** – word of mouth and positive mentions from existing franchisees. Qualtrics report that 93% of consumers say that online reviews influence their purchasing decisions so this one's powerful.
- **Crowd social proof** – you can demonstrate social proof in different ways. For example, a large, authentic following on your social media accounts can give your brand credibility. Alternatively researching industry statistics that can back up why your franchise offering is viable it makes it perceives a lower risk for a prospective franchisee e.g. 25% of every UK household has a dog and the majority of those will need first aid at some point in their lives

gives a really good indication of the demand for learning Dog First Aid.

- **Certification social proof** – third party validation by an industry body of your product or service.

EXERCISE 3

Develop yourself as an industry expert and build the trust your audience has in you by spending 20 minutes a day digging deep on statistics about your industry. Find ways to share them far and wide to add credibility to your franchise offering. Perhaps add one or two to your email signature, include them in eNewsletters or make memes from them for use in your social media.

FRANCHISEE RECRUITMENT ESSENTIALS

5
FAST-TRACKING YOUR FRANCHISEE RECRUITMENT

I WANT you to start thinking about your franchising journey as transforming from a caterpillar to a beautiful butterfly. In the caterpillar phase, you became an expert in delivering your end product or service, whether it was yoga, guitar lessons or French tuition for example. Now, as a franchisor, you are a beautiful butterfly and need to switch your mindset to becoming an expert in running a business that delivers the caterpillar phase expertise.

Next, I want you to take it a step further and think about the brand transformation statement you worked on, and your expertise in helping your ideal franchisees. For example, I'm an expert in helping burnt out, frazzled primary school teachers run a fun and rewarding business. By bringing our mindset in line with our brand transformation statements we can then look at how we can attract those ideal franchisees to our business in large numbers.

Have you ever heard the saying, *your network is your net worth*? Your network at the moment is likely to consist of lots of people who are your franchisees ideal customers rather than your ideal franchisees based on the 4 P's profiling we have covered. You need to build your warm audience of ideal franchisees as well as building the audience of ideal franchisee customers needed to keep the brand growth.

Think of your franchise business as a supplier to the industry of your ideal franchisees. Suppliers join industry bodies to sell to the members. Think about what equivalent you might be able to join or work with in your industry so you can get in front of lots of your ideal franchisees in one hit. For Wizziwoos Kids Clubs, PSHE teachers are a great fit for our brand, so joining the PSHE association is a no brainer. With Dog First Aid, our ideal franchisees were veterinary professionals who wanted a better work/life balance. Attending events like VetFest provided a great opportunity to reach large numbers of our target franchisees with a potential solution that would take them from tired and overwhelmed to leading a fulfilled life running their own profitable business.

A word of caution here. Avoid charging straight in and trying to sell franchises. In my experience, a more successful strategy is to work on getting yourself known, liked and trusted first. Think about how you can add value to the right audiences. You might decide share your “Top 3 tips to avoid burnout when working as a veterinarian” to members of the Royal College of Veterinary Surgeons, if your ideal franchisee is a vet, for example.

There are many routes to finding the ideal franchisee and many experiences to be had along the way.

First of all, franchisee recruitment can take a lot longer than you might expect. Karen Gibb, owner of Mind Marvels says, “It could take just a few weeks to find the right person, or it could take two years or more. This uncertainty can be frustrating, but it's important to be patient and persistent. It's also essential to have a clear idea of what you're looking for in a franchisee, so you don't waste time on candidates who aren't a good fit.

Perhaps the most critical lesson I've learned is the importance of having a clear franchise recruitment roadmap. Prospective franchisees need to know what to expect from the recruitment process and what will happen at each stage. They also need to understand the investment required, the ongoing fees and support, and what they can expect in terms of training and resources. By laying out this information clearly and transparently, we can build trust with our prospects and set them up for success as franchisees.

Franchisee recruitment is a complex process that requires a lot of time, effort, and attention to detail. As the owner of a franchise, it's essential to stay open-minded, patient, and collaborative."

Gibb recalls one particular experience involving her first franchisee: "She came from a financial background and had no experience working directly with kids. I was initially nervous about whether she would be a good fit for our franchise as I was aiming to recruit fellow teachers like myself.

After meeting her, however, I was impressed by her passion for children's wellbeing and her commitment to helping young kids build inner resilience. Despite her lack of experience working with kids, she was eager to learn and embrace the Mind Marvels vision, mission and values. I provided her with extensive training and support, and within a few weeks of opening her franchise, she was running sessions like clockwork!

To my delight, my first franchisee ended up securing multiple school contracts in her first few months of operation. I was pleasantly surprised. Her financial background proved to be a significant asset in negotiating contracts, and her passion for our brand helped her to connect with parents and educators. Her success was a testament to the power of finding franchisees who share our values and are committed to bringing our vision to life.

This experience taught me that, while experience in the children's wellbeing industry is certainly valuable, it's not always necessary. What's most important is finding franchisees who are passionate about our mission and willing to learn and grow with our brand. Sometimes the most unexpected people can become the best franchisees. That's why I'm passionate about recruiting people from all backgrounds."

EXERCISE 4

Carry out some research to understand where your ideal franchisees hang out collectively and spend some time building your "know, like, trust" tactics to help you develop relationships successfully. Think about how the social proof "bandwagon" effect can be applied when getting in front of lots of your franchisees in one go.

Buddy up with industry suppliers who have the same ideal customer profile as you but aren't in direct competition. It may be that you can find ways to work together that benefit both your business and theirs. Perhaps you look at running promotions for each other, take over each other's social media platforms for a day or maybe you share a stand at an event.

6
FRANCHISE MARKETING MOJO

The quick easy hack in this section is one that I have developed, tested and tweaked personally. I tested a lot of different tactics and measured the results of each.

To give you some background, I began my first franchise while I was a single mum of two. I was running two businesses and time was precious. The financial pressures were high as these businesses provided all my income. There were bills to pay, children to support who wanted ballet, hip hop, piano lessons and much more, and I needed to find as many shortcuts and hacks as I could to maximise the impact of the marketing that I was doing. I did a lot of learning and there were many 5 a.m. starts to get work done before the children woke up and the day-to-day working "in" the businesses rather than "on" them started.

Repurposing a piece of work into lots of different formats as listed below is time and energy efficient. You can use it for years to come when done strategically.

A website called answerthepublic.com allows you to generate key search terms for the topic of your choosing. For example, 'burnout primary teacher' will return over 30 search terms that are being searched for around this such as "are primary school teachers in demand in the UK" and "why teachers quit UK". You can use each term as a blog post heading and incorporate several of the search terms in your copy. This will make your website more 'Google-friendly', optimising it for search by prospective franchisees. You can then use that blog post as a foundation for lots of other content.

Here are some of the different assets I created from one blog post:

- An educational video
- Several bitesize videos

- Audio recording of the blog
- Video using the audio and eye-catching visuals (I use Canva for this)
- Memes using excerpts
- Social media headlines
- Podcast topic

I have found that having four content pillars always gives me something to speak about. I define a content pillar as an overarching topic that will add value to my ideal customer.

For example, with Franchise Business School, my four content pillars are:

1. Franchisee business vision
2. Franchisor wellbeing
3. Franchisee recruitment
4. Franchising education

EXERCISE 5:

Identify four marketing channels which enable you to get in front of your ideal franchisees.

7
THE SALES FUNNEL

My six-step Franchisee Sales Funnel is a tried and tested method of structuring the process of selling franchises. The key is to integrate it as part of your strategy so that you keep an abundance of inbound warm leads coming into the top of the funnel. The more you bring in at the top, the more will naturally come out of the bottom.

Here are your six steps in more detail.

1. **Build a warm audience**

Know who you want to attract to your offering and position yourself as an expert / supplier to their industry. Ideally, this step will happen at the beginning of your franchising journey, before you've even franchised and while you are going through the franchising process. This ensures you are building a following and a database of people who know, like and trust you and your brand. Not just any people though; this should be a strategic move to get in front of those you have identified as your ideal franchisees, as opposed to those who are the current ideal customers for the business you are franchising. You shouldn't stop doing the latter, but by doing the former you are warming them up, ready to sell to them when the time is right.

Many franchisors I work with go in at step 2 below and skip step 1 completely. What happens then is they are trying to sell franchises to people they haven't yet built a relationship with. Absolutely you can do this, but there is greater logic in building a following of people you want to sell to in the future, getting their eyes on your brand, adding value to them and attracting their attention to your next moves. Don't worry, I'm not talking about taking everyone who could be a potential franchisee out for lunch. You simply have to create a compound effect of showing up consistently in their space, preferably where you can find them hanging out collectively online or in person. This way you can reduce your marketing spend because you are showing up to many rather than one at a time.

Building that "know, like, trust" effect is so important. Imagine someone you don't know trying to sell you something before you know who they are or what their business is about. You might have seen a bit about their business but you don't know them at all. I'm sure you've had people slide in to your social media messages doing this. On the other hand, if it's someone you know and have built up a rapport with over time, trying to sell something to you, you are more likely to interact with them and want to find out more about their offering.

Building relationships and warming your audience up to sell to can take 6-12 months, so start planting those seeds as early as possible in your franchising journey. You don't need a prospectus or any offering to do this. All you need to do is identify who your ideal franchisees are, understand where they hang out, and be clear about what you are helping them with. Then add value to them. Let them get to know you. Inject oodles of your personality into everything you do with your business. You can hold your warm audience wherever you like – perhaps in a Facebook group or online community. I recommend introducing a step during your audience-building that encourages them to sign up for something that adds value to capture their contact details. If you identify your ideal franchisees as accountants for example, you could share your "Top 10 tips to help time-poor accountants achieve a better balance" in a beautiful eBook or a video. This can help increase their feelings of trust towards you. Don't use it as a sales pitch, just make it helpful and add a little section about you and your business at the end.

2. **Prospectus download**

Have a clean and clear franchise page on your website, or a website dedicated to your franchise business, where prospects can enter their contact details to download your Franchise Prospectus (also known as your Franchise Information Memorandum). First impressions count. Inject personality into your Prospectus and use statistics and testimonials.

Your Franchise Prospectus should be reviewed annually with updates that include recent industry statistics to evidence brand viability and longevity, fresh imagery and current testimonials from franchisees and customers alike. Examine your Prospectus with a critical eye. Ask yourself what has changed and developed in the business that could be seen as beneficial to a prospective franchisee coming on board? What makes your Prospectus different to others? Recognise there are different learning styles and those reading your Prospectus will not perceive your messages in the same way. Think about how you could incorporate different learning styles into your Prospectus. Make it as easy for your prospective franchisees to understand your messages.

3. **The 15 minute call**

You will ideally have a drip campaign set up to follow the download of the Prospectus. This is a series of 5-10 emails that are automatically sent out in pretty quick succession over the following two weeks with a strong, simple and clear call to action in each, encouraging the prospect to get in touch. These automated emails shouldn't be relied upon however. Some will go into spam folders and some franchisees may feel like another number on a database somewhere rather than a valued enquiry. A way around this is to put a system in place where there is human intervention in your sales process early on post-enquiry. When prospects sign up for the Prospectus in step 2, capture a contact number and their postcode too, so you can reach out to them in other ways. A 15 minute call can make sure they have received the Prospectus and give you an opportunity to ask key questions to ensure they meet your basic franchisee criteria.

The key questions help you gather essential basic information about their needs, which may or may not help them meet your criteria. For example, do they need a driving license and do they have one? These questions ensure you don't waste any more of your time or theirs if they're not the right fit. The call can also be used to schedule a longer 45 minute call. They may have many questions of their own to ask. When a franchisee enquiries about a franchise opportunity, they are very much thinking about it from their personal perspective and not yet able to see the franchisor's point of view. Investing in your brand is a very big decision for them – life-changing in fact. What prospective franchisees may fail to see initially is that it is also a big decision for the franchisor taking a franchisee on and that you won't just accept anyone who has the money to come in. You don't want to scare them away, but it is valuable to start planting the seed that it is a two way decision whether or not they come on board, not just theirs. This can also create a greater desire in the prospect for something they now know they might not be able to have.

1. **The 45 minute call**

This call provides an opportunity to interview the prospect for your franchising offering, as well as going into more depth answering their questions. As part of this step you need to make sure they are clear about how they will fund the initial investment, how they will pay ongoing franchise fees and able to give you an overview of the finances. If you are going to do a Discovery Day, include cashflow forecasts and territory mapping as part of it. If you are not including Discovery Days as part of your funnel, provide prospects with this information prior to the call so you can go through it all together. Also make sure to ask how they propose to fund the new venture in Step 3. Really dig into why they are looking to buy in to your brand and what their motivation is. Would coming on board as a franchisee with you solve a problem for them? This is what you can then focus on helping them with.

4. **Discovery Day**

Discovery Days are a great way to showcase your offering whether they are virtual or in person. They are not an essential part of the funnel, but they can be a great tool to increase conversion from prospect to franchisee. Discovery Days also give you something tangible with which to move the sales process along and keep the prospective franchisee focused on the next step. Make them as interactive as possible and get them to feel part of your community. You can create a buzz around marketing them which I go in to more detail later. The Day gives you an opportunity to get to know prospects better but without the pressure of a one-to-one, so they are able to relax more. You can ask them to introduce themselves to the group and even do a short presentation to get an idea of their confidence level. Seeing how they interact in this way can make it easier for you to see personalities more clearly and know whether they are a good fit for the brand. Not all franchise leads will need to go to a Discovery Day. With practice, you will be able to judge each lead on its own merits and get some sales closed and signed off before a Discovery Day.

5. **Deposit and franchise agreement**

When you have made a decision about whether or not you are happy for the prospect to come on board, you can take a deposit. This shows intent to proceed and makes the prospective franchisee put their money where their mouth is. Until the full balance is paid and the Franchise Agreement signed, that franchise territory is not yet sold. The prospect should therefore not have access to any operations manuals, systems and processes or anything they need to actually run the business until the full amount is paid and the Franchise Agreement signed. However, you can give them a "behind the scenes" peak on the Discovery Day, to show them what they can expect. Perhaps even show them the contents page of the Operations Manual, but no more than that. Send the Franchise Agreement to them. If you are running a Discovery Day you'll be able to highlight these next steps at the end of the session. Not all franchisors take a deposit; some move straight on to sending the Franchise Agreement out. I have always favoured taking a deposit as it is a psychological commitment on the part of the incoming franchisee, as well as providing me as the franchisor with a layer of security. You could also ask the prospective franchisee to sign an Intent to Commit document. There needs to be clarity between all parties whether or not the deposit is refundable should they not proceed. All prospective franchisees should be advised to get their Franchise Agreement reviewed by a solicitor specialising in franchises prior to signing.

Note: Before sharing any brand secrets or financial information, get the prospective franchisee to sign a Non-Disclosure Agreement (NDA). This not only protects your business, but also your franchisees businesses, AND reassures the prospective franchisee that you take the protection of their future business seriously.

Ultimately, the clearer you are about your ideal franchisee profile and the more your messaging resonates with them, the higher the quality of warm audience you will be able to build. To summarise, the more you have in the top of the funnel, the more will come out at the bottom.

8
FRANCHISEE SALES NUMBERS

THE ANSWER'S USUALLY in the numbers somewhere with business.

Find a way that works for you to log each step of the sales funnel numbers, along with any associated notes, evaluation and self-critique. I have white boards dotted about all over the place but am also a fan of a good spreadsheet. I know I won't always look at my spreadsheets, so I have the key overarching numbers on my whiteboards so I can't help but see them.

The key to successful implementation of the sales funnel is to know your numbers and measure the metrics at each stage. With each step of the funnel there will be fewer and fewer people filtering through the steps. By regularly evaluating the process, you can identify any bottlenecks where the numbers drop significantly, and look for ways in which you can increase the conversion rate to the next stage. A usual franchisee sales conversion rate from lead to sale is circa 1-3%, however, this is based on *not* having a warm audience already built ready to launch to.

Keep it super simple to help you stay on track.

Ask yourself what you did that made a difference to the numbers, regardless of whether that difference had a positive or a negative impact.

Use the tools available to you to collate data in the background. Two of my favourites are Facebook Pixels and Google Analytics. Set them up and make a note in your calendar to review them every month, comparing your figures to the month before. These tools build data for you to analyse. The intelligence they collect can tell you everything from the demographics of the people looking at your "stuff" down to what day and time is most popular for your audience to do so. You can see what elements of your marketing are working – or not –to help you be more strategic.

Have you heard of Pareto's law? It's all based round the 80/20 principle where 20% of doing something will get you 80% of your results. The tools available to us enable us to identify which 20% of our marketing is getting us 80% of our results, so we can do more of it.

The 80/20 rule can be applied to most areas of life and business. Without measuring the metrics though, you won't know what 20% to focus on.

9
YOUR FRANCHISE MARKETING STRATEGY

YOUR MARKETING STRATEGY should go hand-in-hand with the top of your sales funnel. Your marketing should be based on getting the right people into your warm audience. It is entirely up to you, and where you are at with your franchise at the moment, as to how you build your strategy. Franchisors who are right at the beginning of their journey and have just spent thousands going through the franchising process might not have the budget available to do large overarching national marketing campaigns. As you build a larger network of franchisees, more budget will become available for this. Check out the next chapter for more information on national marketing budgets.

The lower budget, local marketing strategy is where most franchisors need to focus in the initial stages to first sell pilot franchises, then full price ones in order to build up the national marketing budget pot. It can also be useful to have your pilot franchisees closer to home so you are able to give them more hands on support in the early days should they need it. The purpose of having pilot franchisees at all is to iron out any teething problems and make sure the Operations Manual is tight and an accurate reflection of the business you have franchised. Being able to work closely with your pilots helps you streamline systems and processes as much as possible, paving the way for future franchisees coming in and creating further proof that the business is a low risk investment. You can also use your pilot franchisees effectively as a focus group to find out where you can find more prospects like them.

Targeted marketing in the local area is really important when you are looking at your ten year vision. This helps you avoid taking a "spray and pray" approach to your marketing and makes it easier to condense your budget as opposed to spreading it thinly only to have a lower impact. You will be marketing to people who are likely to have been exposed to your brand in some regard as you have already built a business in that area.

As we discussed earlier in the book, I recommend having four key content pillars to help you structure your marketing. Pick four areas you could talk about until the cows come home and then mind-map them out. I am old-school and like to get my coloured pens out and use either the back of a section of old wallpaper or an A3 pad, but there are also lots of mind map tools available online that you can use too such as Coggle, MindMeister or Ayoa. I make a big circle with the topic I am exploring in the middle and then with my different colour pens I draw branches coming away from the centre, leading to ideas. Every time I get stuck, I change colour pen and suddenly more ideas flow. If I get really stuck, then Google or Chat GPT is always on hand too but I love the creativity and authenticity of mind-mapping with good old pen and paper. Off the back of this exercise, I repurpose content in different ways – blog posts, social media memes, press releases, and videos, to give me enough content for a year and then some.

Key parts of your strategy should be building the know, like and trust, showing credibility and adding value to the warm audience you are building at the top of your funnel. Everything you are putting out about your franchise should be worded appropriately for your ideal franchisees. Think of yourself as a farmer planting lots of seeds and watering them ready for a bountiful harvest. These activities are usually free or low-cost and super-powerful in laying firm foundations for future franchise sales.

You need to ask for an expression of interest before selling to your audience. Then add value until your warm audience is ready to sell to. For example, "This is what I'm going to share with you today, and then after, if it's ok with you, I'd like to tell you a bit more about some business opportunities I've got available." That way you are getting consent to sell to them and it doesn't feel sleazy or icky when it comes to it – just a naturally smooth transition that's expected.

10
NATIONAL MARKETING BUDGETS

Most franchises will have a national marketing budget built in as part of the Franchise Agreement. This means that either a set amount or a percentage of turnover will be paid to the franchisor separately to the ongoing franchise fees, for national marketing. These monies need to be used in line with the description detailed in the Franchise Agreement signed by the franchisee.

Generally, you can carry out activities on a national scale with these monies that promote the brand. It may be a Google AdWords campaign, a Meta marketing campaign, an exhibition, or a stand at a relevant show.

The more the brand grows, the more it adds to the individual franchise territories. Paying into the national marketing budget pot is therefore beneficial to all involved, provided it is correctly spent. Franchisees need to be able to see the value in handing over monies that they have worked their butts off to earn in their businesses, or it can create an environment where you have disgruntled franchisees feeling undervalued.

Usually, it states in the Franchise Agreement that the national marketing budget needs to be accounted for separately from the usual franchise business revenue. This is absolutely best practice. If a franchisee ever asks what the budget is being spent on it is also much easier to show them the income and expenditure from a separate account, or a separate nominal code report that you can pull from your book-keeping software. Transparency around national marketing budgets is important and ethical.

11
PAID MARKETING

As a franchisor and a leader in business it is important to be strategic with paid marketing to maximise the results and return on investment. There are of course many platform marketing experts and PR gurus who can guide you. When you're a new franchisor though, the budget isn't always there for you to spend thousands on this kind of resource.

I've summarised my learnings and experiences with the two main online advertising platforms below.

Google AdWords

This platform has historically worked well for me with excellent customer support. They have jumped on calls, shared screens, taken over my screen and been genuinely helpful in maximising the results from my ad spend with them. Google's representatives clearly explain how to use negative and positive key words, ensuring that money is only spent on the positive key words – search terms that my ideal franchisees might use. The data and metrics around your ad spend is clearly presented in a user-friendly format that means you can read your data and tweak your campaigns effectively.

Meta

Meta is the brand behind Facebook. With this platform, I haven't personally found the same level of customer support. However, this is a powerful tool and not to be overlooked.

Testing and measuring the results of the copy, imagery and links that you are using in your ads is important. Many experts advise to use smaller budgets initially while you test different executions and learn the ropes. See what pulls in the best results with just a £5 per day budget for three days. You need to be able to measure the results at each stage of your funnel. Start by writing copy for 3-5 adverts, scroll through all the images you could use on your mobile and see which ones catch your eye and stop you scrolling. Then, match your copy with an image (or video), then pick two and test them alongside each other. The one that pulls the best click through rates, engagement or franchise enquiries (depending on the advert goal I am measuring for that advert) is tested alongside another. The winner is tested alongside another. Repeat this 3-5 times. I don't profess to be a paid Meta advert expert at all. I have placed many and many successfully however they are notoriously tricky to understand. Facebook have their own online help section with extensive guidance specifically about this on their website.

There are some great franchise publications that claim to have fantastic reach. However, interrogate these closely and bear in mind these publications need to generate income through advertising and their job is to sell advertising opportunities to you. Also question whether or not their reader is your ideal customer. Would the money they are asking for be better spent on getting in front of your ideal franchisees another way? In my experience, there are lower-cost options available until you have a large budget and are confident that the odds of a reward outweigh the expense required.

Publications

If you are looking to include publications as part of your paid marketing strategy, then industry publications are a good place to start. By industry publications, I mean the industry that you have identified your current franchisee is already working in before they come on board. For example, *Vet Times Magazine* made a suitable publication for Dog First Aid. This may be the sweet spot where you are delving in to an area that most franchisors aren't, because they are advertising through franchise publications. But, you know exactly who you want to have on board as a franchisee after you've done the 4 P's exercise, so you can go directly to the industries your prospects are currently working in as suppliers. You are supplying ideal candidates with a solution to a problem they are currently facing.

Directories

Online directories provide another way to increase your visibility. There are many free directories and some that charge a small fee. Find larger competitors who have the same or similar target audiences as you, Google them and see where they are showing up online, then register with the same directories. With children's activities, there are sites like *Mumsnet* and *NetMums* you can list on. All of these contribute to your digital footprint and help build a catalogue of back links to your website, which in turn helps optimise your website for search.

Awards

Sponsoring awards is another option but prices can vary. If you have a budget for paid marketing, sponsoring awards in your industry could be a great way to increase your visibility and get in front of the right audience. This is a fun way to spend your budget. You recognise exemplary performance and usually have a meal and a few drinks thrown in too. In the lead-up to the awards event the organisers usually mention their sponsors to their audiences – your ideal franchisees – in their communication. You can network with the other award sponsors who often have the same ideal customer but are not in direct competition, providing possible opportunities to collaborate in future.

There are many specific franchise industry events to explore, each facilitating social gatherings and great opportunities to network with other franchisors and industry professionals. These are great for networking with peers, and have been game-changers for me personally in finding others who understand my position, making life-long friends along the way. Supporting these events, other franchisors and the industry as a whole is a fabulous way to give back and raise your profile within the franchise industry. Newer franchisors who are not yet making their business break even from the ongoing franchise fees – the bread and butter of their franchise businesses – may want to think more strategically about how they spend any budget allocated to award sponsorship. To sell franchises, we are not usually looking to market to this audience of franchise peers; we are looking at our ideal franchisee profile and where they might be attending awards so we can get in front of them.

Top Tip!

Beware of organisations that may call you claiming they will get you to the top of the Google search page if you give them thousands of pounds.

This is nothing you can't do yourself with a little research, time and consistency. Some suppliers assume that, as a franchisor, you have a magic money tree that pops up at the end of the garden. They don't understand that many new franchisors are actually juggling two businesses and using the income from the original business – the business they have franchised – to keep the franchise business afloat.

12
FREE AND LOW-COST MARKETING

Anyone already familiar with your brand has already built a rapport with your business. Focussing your attention on who is already in your network, who has been a customer past or present, who your current suppliers are, who is watching your content on social media and who you are already connected with, costs nothing.

People usually like to help people. Asking those in your audience and email lists if they can take a couple of minutes to share something for you. It costs nothing. You may have people in your audience who work in organisations with intranets, such as the NHS or local authorities, who might be able to advertise your business.

It's a visibility game of getting your offering in front of as many people as possible, strategically.

Newsletters

Newsletters can be free or low-cost depending on the platform you use and the number of people on your list. I have used Mailchimp, MadMimi and Mailerlite myself but many others are out there. Getting regular newsletters out to your audience, and making sure you are in people's inboxes positioning as an expert will help keep you at the forefront of their minds. I recommend doing this monthly at least, but preferably weekly or bi-weekly. You can batch-create newsletters to make the workload easier, but many people prefer to do it ad hoc. I know some who spend a day at the beginning of each year drafting their newsletter content for the next 12 months. They write an article, then schedule it to go out on their websites as a blog. The link from the blog is then embedded in the newsletter so that the first few lines of text show with a link to "read more" directing them to the website to read the full article as a blog post. This means the website traffic is increased by sending people from their email to your site.

Don't worry about people unsubscribing. Some people take it personally when they are notified that someone has unsubscribed from their email list. They have done you a favour and naturally decluttered themselves, saving you time and energy from following up on a lead that isn't interested.

Newsletters are not only a great way of building your audience but also a way of letting those on your list get to know you and your brand. Having something to "exchange" for their email address is key to attracting the right people to your list. You ideally want to be building a list of people who match your ideal franchisee profile. To attract your ideal people, you can offer something free to download that adds value and positions you as an expert. Of course, having an option on your website for those interested in becoming a franchisee to download your Franchise Prospectus is great and provides you with a condensed list of interested parties to sell to. However, to hook in the wider audience of ideal franchisees, it makes sense to have a free gift for them that helps with where they are now and of course more information about you and your franchise offering at the end. For example, with Wizziwoos Kids

Clubs, PSHE teachers are a fabulous fit for the brand, so a free guide titled "3 Top Tips to help PSHE Teachers Avoid Burnout" might be of value. We then know that those who download the guide are PSHE teachers who are feeling like they may be at risk of burnout and therefore could be looking for alternative ways to use their qualifications and skillsets. Once they are in the list they form part of the warm audience for email marketing.

Social media

This is a great free way to get in front of your ideal franchisees, if you know where they are. For example, with our alpaca business, Facebook is a sweet spot. If I could replicate the organic reach and engagement that I get from our alpaca business Facebook page across my other businesses, it would be a dream. Instagram, however, isn't so great for this business. This surprised me as it is a more visual platform, so I had assumed that lots of pictures of the alpacas would go down a storm there. Instagram is great for Wizziwoos Kids Clubs however, but Facebook not so much. For Franchise Business School, LinkedIn and Facebook groups are the two platforms that currently pull the best results. You need to know your numbers and work on measuring the metrics. Give people something to talk about. They need to have their eyes on your brand and it needs to be visible. Have a think about where your ideal franchisees hang out online and make it your new favourite place to be. Add heaps of value and genuinely attempt to build relationships.

Email marketing

Directly emailing businesses at the time of writing is GDPR compliant, however, targeting individuals with emails designed to sell is not acceptable. There is a great platform called GMass which can help you in this. At the time of writing, GMass allows you to send 50 free emails a day in one hit by syncing your GMail account with a Google Sheet that contains a list of the emails you are sending to. There are reasonably priced payment plans available too which allow you to send even more. As usual, the answer's in the numbers and by monitoring the comprehensive analytics that you are able to tap in to using GMass, you are able to hone your email marketing and use more of the copy that readers react to. Perhaps you can see that out of 100 emails sent, 30 downloaded the prospectus, 15 of which you got on a call, five went through to a Discovery Day and one went on to buy a franchise. You then know that for every 100 emails you send out, you stand a good chance of selling a franchise territory.

Blog posts

Posts on your own website are a great way to repurpose content, as we've already discussed. Sometimes, I find writing blog posts a bit of a mind-over-matter thing. I plug in my noise cancelling head phones and switch off all the notifications on my phone. I have to really avoid procrastination on this one for some reason. It is such a golden piece of the jigsaw puzzle though, as the copy you write is good for years to come and can be used in so many different ways.

Phone calls

Picking up the telephone seems to be something people shy away from more and more, which makes it more valuable to those who still doing it. If someone has given you their contact number, you have permission to call them. Capture this on your Prospectus download form so you can get in there and speak to them. Don't hide behind your keyboard! Even if you just send a text message, you are head and shoulders above the rest. According to a Textsanity article in July 2022, 98% of text messages delivered are opened (90% of those within three minutes), as opposed to typically only 20% of emails. This is obviously a medium not to be sniffed at with statistics like that. WhatsApp is my preferred medium for texting/messaging as I can see whether or not the message has been delivered and then whether or not it's been read.

Vehicle livery

This can work well for some businesses. Obviously, if your car is an old rust bucket of a farm vehicle that is often covered in muck, like mine currently is, then it may not portray your business in the best light. If you have a half-decent car or van however, this may be a useful option. You can also strategically park it in areas where you are looking to next sell a territory, with a plastic leaflet holder that hooks on the window with some leaflets inside. Parking it near where your ideal franchisee works could help them see it on their way to work. Or, if you have profiled them well enough, you'll know which supermarkets they frequent and roughly what times they shop, so you can make sure your car is there for them to see, with leaflets for them to grab around that time. Make sure your vehicle livery clearly states that you have franchise opportunities available. Wherever you go, you will then be marketing just by driving your car.

Press releases

These can be useful as long as they are successful in being featured in a publication that your ideal franchisee will read. Some publications will commit to running your press release in return for a fee or alongside a paid ad. Each opportunity needs to be judged on its own merits. I personally like to wait for something newsworthy to happen or make something happen in the business, such as an award win or a new franchisee recruited, so I have a little more to say.

13
MAKING IT EASY FOR POTENTIAL FRANCHISEES TO CHOOSE YOU

We live in a digital age and everyone wants things now. To the point that I have actually caught my daughter standing by the microwave willing it to hurry up. I mean, nothing's going to cook that food any faster, is it? Make it as easy as possible for your potential franchisees to get information about your offering. When a prospective franchisee visits your website it needs to be clear to them where to look to get franchise information, a brief summary or outline, and a "download prospectus" button where you capture their name, email address, phone number and area of interest. It then feeds in to the newsletter platform so you can integrate it with your automated email drip campaign that we discussed in chapter 7. That way, in three clicks they have the information they need.

Nurture your warm audience and keep them interested in your offering. Wherever they hang out, add value to them and continue to build the rapport. If they get to know you, they might not even look at another brand because it's a no brainer for them to buy into your business.

By giving prospects a call promptly after they've downloaded the Prospectus, you can sort out those who are serious about coming on board. Many will be downloading it for information and not in a position to move things forward. Perhaps they are expecting to come into some money from an inheritance or a property sale and are just doing their due diligence at this stage to see whether or not your brand might be the right fit for when those funds drop many months down the line. Getting these prospects on a call and being uber helpful (not salesy or pushy) will help build that "know, like, trust", and a foundation for future sales. Others may simply be being nosey. Then you'll have the serious prospects who are in a position to move forward. Without doing a call or messaging them on WhatsApp they may feel like the franchise is not actually real. You are making personal contact with someone who is passionate about the business opportunity and enthusiastic about the possibilities that it brings. In the initial stages after franchising, it may well be the franchisor who carries out these follow up calls. However, as the franchise grows, it will likely be a member of the Head Office team. Make sure that whoever makes these calls is charismatic with oodles of personality and makes their love for the business infectious to the person they are ringing. How are the prospects supposed to believe in the brand if the person on the end of the phone isn't positive and upbeat about it? Make sure the enthusiasm levels are high and keep in touch with your prospects. Every interaction with the Head Office needs to be a positive one. They will remember how you made them feel. Make them feel good about it.

Show prospective franchisees the journey so that they know what is going to happen next. Use the three "tell 'ems". Tell them what is *going to* happen, tell them what *is happening*, tell them what *happened*. Nothing is a shock to the system then, and they feel well informed at each stage. Be transparent about their revenue projections. If they're not going to make any money in month one, let them know so they are prepared. Don't set them up to fail by giving any false hopes. This level of transparency is an ethical approach to the sales journey that needs to be examined for consistency. Set expectations and over-deliver on them.

14
BRAND MISFITS

Don't be afraid to say no to the wrong fit for your brand. This is something that comes with experience. The first few you sell as a franchisor, you naturally have concerns that they might not be the right fit for your brand, as everything is new for you. Some people will want to come on board but not be in line with your brand values. If they are overly challenging through the process of recruitment, they will likely be difficult after too. I don't mean challenging as in asking reasonable questions that you'd expect and thoroughly doing due diligence. (This should be embraced, as all franchisees should buy in to a brand with their eyes wide open.) I mean being unusually difficult and making demands that you wouldn't expect.

Integrating DISC profiling in to your recruitment process, or using another similar tool, can be a useful way of eliminating potential franchisees that aren't the right fit.

You want to recruit franchisees who are going to take ownership for the business in their area, are accountable for their decisions and take responsibility for decisions in their franchise business, following the brand guidelines. You don't want someone who blames the franchisor when they feel the model isn't working for them, and makes excuses for not having implemented the systems and process correctly, nor someone who is in denial that they are part of a franchise and not out on their own limb.

Strange things happen in franchising that you might not comprehend. Franchisees make decisions sometimes that you don't understand. One that still blows my mind is a lady who bought a territory resale spending just shy of twenty thousand pounds. She was amazing on paper. All the boxes were ticked and she seemed like she could really make her business fly. After training and the initial set-up, I went out and supported her on her first session. She was naturally nervous about delivery but did a fantastic job. A few weeks later, she said she was going to buy herself out of the franchise because it wasn't for her. By the time I'd got back to the office, she'd dropped all of her equipment back and transferred the monies detailed in the Franchise Agreement to negate the remainder of the term of her Agreement.

There will naturally be some misalignments and not everyone will be interested in coming on board. And not all those who come on board, are going to be the right fit. To protect all franchisees' businesses as well as the Head Office business, try to separate the wheat from the chaff early on in your recruitment process. Get as many of the correct franchisees as possible.

Bust any imposter syndrome out of the park. You've built an amazing business to be able to franchise it at all. What your business does will make a big difference to your brand's end users, as well as a massive difference to the franchisees you are onboarding. By keeping that at the heart of your decisions around who comes on board, realising you are only able to do this by staying strong and making informed decisions quickly, you will be able recruit a better quality of franchisee.

Try not to take things personally. I can attest to this. Not only am I a natural introvert and a people pleaser, I also put my heart and soul into my business ventures because I can clearly see the amazing positive impact they have on others. If a franchisee is disgruntled or requires a lot more TLC than I would normally give, I have sometimes taken things to heart. However, it isn't personal. The best way I have found to protect myself and not take things to heart is by having circles of people in my life I can confide in. I first have my "ride and die" circle who I share everything with, then family members and friends who I share most things with but not all. I also have my team, the franchisees and then finally prospective franchisees. It doesn't mean I can't be friendly and nice using this system. I have simply found over the years that it helps me protect myself and stay focussed on business growth and development with those that matter, and not take too many things personally.

That said sometimes business is personal and things do hit hard, but in the words of Winston

Churchill, "When you're going through hell, keep going."

There is a fine balance with the franchisor/franchisee relationship to maintain. It can be tricky if you're too involved in each other's lives to then refuse someone a franchise territory or indeed to pull up an existing franchisee on something in the Franchise Agreement if they won't listen or implement the support and guidance that you have given them.

Most, if not all, franchisors have recruited franchisees that aren't the right fit for the business at some point or another. Some look great on paper and turn out to not be what you expected, while others you're not quite sure about end up soaring high. Making informed decisions and having a defined franchisee recruitment system in place that is regularly updated and tweaked is, in my opinion, the best way to risk mitigate against brand misfits.

DISCOVERY DAYS

15
PROS AND CONS OF DISCOVERY DAYS

PROs

Discovery Days are great to give you the opportunity to get to know potential franchisees at a deeper level. It gives the opportunity to get to know their personalities better, to see how they interact with others, and learn more about their values and their bigger picture plans. You can more easily assess whether they are the kind of person who will take ownership for their decisions and whether they are the right fit for your brand.

Not only is it beneficial for you to get to know your potential franchisees more thoroughly, it also gives them the chance to get to know you better. This builds on the "know, like and trust" between you, your brand and your potential new franchisees. Franchisees are taking a giant leap of faith when they come on board. They are having a huge amount of faith in you and your ability to steer the ship. Discovery Days can expedite the building of trust in the relationship, laying firm foundations for a long and successful business partnership moving forward.

Although traditionally called Discovery Days, these sessions don't necessarily need to be a full day. In fact, many are half days or even just a couple of hours, particularly those that are held online. Some franchisors even record the Discovery Day presentation and simply send the link out when a prospect gets to that stage in their franchisee recruitment process. There are different ways of holding it and it is very much up to you to decide what works best for you and your brand.

Having a set date for your next Discovery Day gives you something that you can tangibly feed enquiries to. When someone enquires, you have qualified them and had a longer call with them, you can feed them on to your next Discovery Day. It can make the sales process more robust and the potential franchisee has to invest a significant amount of time and, in the case of in-person Discovery Days, commit travel time, expense and energy too. It can increase your conversion rate.

You could also use Discovery Days as an opportunity to collect business plans from your prospective franchisees. At the end of the 45 minute call you can issue your prospects with a branded business plan template and ask them to complete and submit it at the Discovery Day. This way they have already had a chance to think how it would look and feel running your business model in their area.

CONs

If you've just had a Discovery Day and you haven't got another one scheduled for a couple of months, there is a risk that a prospect goes cold and looks elsewhere in between.

Discovery Days may also be something that are outside of your comfort zone, but also something that is outside of your prospects' comfort zone. Are social skills, standing up in front of people, being bubbly and outgoing, interacting on different levels and being personable, elements that a franchisee coming on board with your brand will need in order to successfully run the business model? If so, then it might be that Discovery Days are a great way forward as it gives showcase opportunities to prospective franchisees to help you make a decision about whether they are the right fit.

Planning a Discovery Day can be time consuming. You need at least six weeks prior to the Discovery Day to do an effective build up. The weeks before and after the Discovery Day ideally need to be blocked out in your diary to allow you to focus on intense marketing and post-Discovery Day follow up.

16
WHERE TO HOLD YOUR DISCOVERY DAYS

If you have your own premises you can of course hold your Discovery Day at your own offices. However, many franchisors start by working from a home office, the sofa or even the cupboard under the stairs. Perhaps you do have offices but don't feel they would be suitable to impress and accurately represent the brand impression you would like to portray.

In these scenarios you could look at renting an office space, meeting room or boardroom. You might choose to do this in a location that is more central, to make the Discovery Day more easily accessible to a more franchisees. There are several suppliers to the franchise industry who offer office space to franchisors for Discovery Days and new franchisee training at no or low cost which may be an option. You can outsource catering or order in platters of food from supermarkets if the venue doesn't provide the option.

The cheapest option for a Discovery Day is to hold it online via a platform like Zoom or Teams. It is easier, cheaper and less time-consuming. However, it may not give you the energy and interaction levels you can get in person. You can use the chat box to encourage interaction to a certain extent. In my opinion, virtual Discovery Days are a secondary option to in-person, should budgets or geographical constraints be a block. Being in the same room as other prospects, looking people in the eye, going round the room and seeing how they interact with each other, actively listening and really hearing their stories in person, to me is more powerful.

17

HOW TO INVITE PROSPECTS

Holding a Discovery Day means you have something tangible to promote. You can list the Discovery Day as an event on social media platforms, and in the areas that your ideal franchisee hangs out online. It's something you can physically put out into the world and promote. It's a way of saying "Hey, this is us and we can't wait to have heaps of fun with you on our Discovery Day where we will show you how to change your life by being part of our brand".

You can of course invite any previous franchise enquirers to attend the Discovery Day, but you can also use their emails to create a "look-a-like" audience to retarget on social media. This allows you to create an advert that targets people like them.

Tap on the shoulder invites are effective too. They can be seen as more personal because you message prospects individually and invite them to attend, perhaps using a voice note or a video message to show you value them as an individual, rather than it being another "copy and paste" message they are receiving.

18
WHO SHOULD ATTEND A DISCOVERY DAY

Particularly in the early days of franchising, you, the franchisor, should attend the Discovery Day. Your passion and enthusiasm for the business will shine through. You can explain first-hand how you started the business and the key elements of what's involved.

Any Head Office team members that franchisees regularly come into contact with could be in attendance. Perhaps you have someone who helps with the on-boarding process, or a dedicated team member to provide franchisee support. It is very dependent on the structure of the business and where you're at in your franchising journey.

If you have existing franchisees who accurately represent the brand with enthusiasm, invite them along as well. Consider giving them a little gift to thank them for their time. People attending the Discovery Day can then speak to someone who has been where they are now, happily running their own successful business. This also continues to build the know, like, trust elements, meaning that the franchisee can see that you and your brand are trustworthy through this third part validation.

I had my mentor attend the first few Discovery Days. I actually held the first few at his offices. He gave a short talk as part of the day about the importance of franchisor support in a franchise network so I was then able to confirm how those areas were met under my business model. It was reassuring to have him there to give me a bit of confidence and to have him as my cheerleader. The first couple of times I ran a Discovery Day, it was completely outside of my comfort zone, so I found this really useful.

19
WHAT TO INCLUDE IN A DISCOVERY DAY PRESENTATION

So, what should you include in your presentation on the day itself? A combination of important information about the brand, testimonials, social proof and statistics. You can create a presentation that you can use for both face to face and virtual discovery days. Sprinkle lots of high quality imagery preferably where eye contact by the human (or animal) is being made to evoke an emotion in attendees.

Contents

Don’t forget to have regular breaks and make sure that your prospects are aware of what the structure of the day will be. Explain where the fire exits and toilets are. Advise exactly when the breaks will be, as well as the time you intend the Discovery Day to finish. Let them know you'll be around afterwards to answer any questions they have. Make them feel comfortable in the environment they are in – they are with new people in a strange place, so are outside of their comfort zones. They need to feel welcomed.

Introductions

I always find introductions really useful for assessing prospects' suitability for the role of being a franchisee with my Dog First Aid franchise prospects. Providing training classes in dog first aid requires standing in front of a room full of strangers with confidence and delivering high quality content. If prospective franchisees were able to do this at Discovery Day stage and introduce themselves to others in the room, preferably with a sprinkle of humour added in, then I knew they had good potential to represent my brand. There would be alarm bells ringing for anyone who wasn't able to tick this box.

Start by introducing anyone in the room who isn't a prospective franchisee then give each person attending the opportunity to introduce themselves to the room. Give them a brief outline of what to talk about, for example their name, location of interest, what they do now, funniest memory from the last year (to break the ice.)

What is the franchise?

Introduce your brand to them including any achievements, no matter how small. Include how the franchise came about and why it was founded. Was it because you saw a gap in the market, or felt passionately about something and wanted to make a difference?

Third party associations / memberships

Provide details of any third party associations or memberships. If you work alongside any organisations or are accredited.Talk through what each one is and what the benefits of association/membership are. If you've won any awards talk about those too.

Case study

Let the prospective franchisees see who they will be helping by running a business under your umbrella by inserting a customer case study. Describe how your product or service has helped a customer using words that capture the emotions felt by the customer before they used your product or service and how they feel now. Prospects need to see the potential for the difference they will be able to make to people by running your model in their local area.

Testimonials

Pop in screenshots of customer testimonials so that they can see that the testimonials are authentic. Try and find ones that give them a "wow".

What the franchise does

This is the section where you describe the products and services a franchisee is able to offer their potential customers in their local area. For example, my business Wizziwoos Kids Clubs makes finance fun through our school holiday and half term clubs for primary school age children.

How do we do it?

The nitty gritty of a franchisee's business, including the times they would offer the product or service, and what preparation might look like before they can deliver the product or service.

Why franchise?

Did you franchise to reach more people with your end product or service? Or perhaps it was to keep up with demand? Maybe it was a combination of both, or could it be because you wanted to help other people have the level of work life balance running a business they love that you have achieved with your special brand formula? Consider including a quote about being stronger together from someone renowned in business or in your industry.

Franchisee testimonial

If you already have some franchisees on board, insert some franchisee testimonial videos, text and / or case studies with images. If you don't but you do have team members helping you with your business put something from them in that details how they love the brand and that shows you aren't an ogre to be in business with. With an in-person discovery day where you have a lunch break and existing franchisees in attendance, prospects have the opportunity to pick their brains and chat to them informally which is invaluable.

What can I expect as a franchisee?

Reassure them they won't just pay their initial lump sum fee and you will be off running for the hills. Explain what initial training and ongoing support looks like in your brand. Show them the back end of any franchisee portals you have. (Disclaimer: ALWAYS make sure a non-disclosure agreement is signed by anyone attending the Discovery Day.) Describe where they can access support and how quickly after coming on board they will be able to access everything. Tell them when the next training dates are for new franchisees and advise how soon after their training they will be able to start running their new business and get money coming in.

A day in the life of a franchisee

If you can insert a video here too, that's fantastic. It doesn't need to be a video shadowing a franchisee, it could be you that it is shadowing, as you go about the day-to-day activities a franchisee would undertake when running their own business with your brand. This section combined with the cashflow forecast examples slide below can paint a powerful picture to prospective franchisees of what their lives could look like, along with the income levels that are achievable when the model is followed.

Cashflow forecast examples

Show them the basic income and expenditure that a franchisee could earn. Do not over-inflate these. It is better to set realistic expectations than to promise they'll be millionaires this time next year. You are potentially going to be in a business relationship with these people for years to come, so transparency and honesty is key. Ensure you have a disclaimer detailing that any financials are subject to the franchisee's actions, with them taking liability for the financials of their business, and that the cashflow forecasts are for illustration purposes.

What makes us different?

Detail how your unique selling point differentiates you from other businesses in your sector.

Key attributes you are looking for

What is it that makes an ideal franchisee for your brand? It could be experience, values, integrity, ability to deliver excellent presentations, organisation skills, self-motivation. Such attributes will be unique to your brand.

Why the franchise works

Prove to your prospects that the business model is viable. Use statistics from the industry you are operating in, or research that has been carried out by third party sources, to demonstrate this. Also include some franchise industry statistics, perhaps from the most recent NatWest & British Franchise Association Survey. This supports why franchising is a great business model. Always reference the source of the statistics you use.

Your investment

Detail the amount prospects would need to invest in order to come on board. Are there different options for them to choose from? How much is the equipment package? Could they get a discount if they come on board within a certain time frame post-Discovery Day?

Next steps

Advise prospects of how things will progress from this stage on. Are you taking a deposit? When can they pay that? You're making the decision to come on board a no-brainer. This is what their life could look like. This is what they could be earning. This is why this franchise is the one for them. This is why the model works and why franchising is awesome. This is the pathway to making it a reality. Explain that prospects can build their franchise as an asset for resale. It's not money lost; it's an investment.

Have fun on your Discovery Day. It's contagious! Get some awesome prizes in and pose a mini-challenge through which they can win something. For example, the first person to post a selfie / video with #(insert your brand name)discoveryday wins a prize. Leave the prospects with a sense that being part of your franchise will be a positive experience they'll enjoy. Attendees will always remember how you made them feel. Usually, people look to come on board as a franchisee because they are not enjoying what they are doing currently. By demonstrating that your brand is fun to be part of will speak volumes, as well as helping you to relax.

At the end of the day, hand out a feedback form or provide a link to a digital form and ask attendees to fill it in there and then. Ask leading questions about how future Discovery Days can be improved or better marketed. Examples of questions you could ask include:

- What are your top 3 takeaways from today's session?
- What did you enjoy most about the Discovery Day?
- How do you feel you benefited from attending today?

Have an email scheduled in which you can insert some of the quotes from the feedback forms and hit send the evening of the Discovery Day or the day after.

20
MARKETING YOUR DISCOVERY DAY

Having a process or a timeline to market your Discovery Day strategically is crucial. I have prepared a Gantt chart that you can access at subscribepage.com/theganttchart. The first time using it can be quite intense, just as the first time you carry out anything new. You will need to draft copy, social media assets and email templates. However, after the first time, you can roll it out again and again. This is intense franchisee recruitment marketing and I would recommend you clear your work diary as best you can the week before the Discovery Day and the week after, so that your only focus is the Discovery Day with as few distractions as possible.

Preparation is key!

Use the process and timeline in the Gantt chart by inserting the appropriate dates starting with the date of your Discovery Day and working backwards.

The Gantt chart lays out step-by-step exactly what you need to do with a comprehensive six week plan.

Metrics

Track all your key numbers at the start of marketing and at the end of the week after your Discovery Day. The answer is always in the numbers. By tracking your numbers, you are able to identify any funnel blocks and adjust to reduce them.

Objectives

Many people focus solely on the goal to recruit more franchisees and get closer to achieving financial results. You should absolutely do this and I'd recommend having a low-hanging goal, or a good, better and best goal for your recruitment figures or revenue gain from the Discovery Day. It may be that your low hanging goal is 0 for the first time you run a day like this, so you are definitely going to achieve it. That's absolutely fine! You make the rules.

I recommend having other goals as well as the recruitment goals so you learn from the process of rolling out the Discovery Day marketing process. Learning goals maybe to identify which copy and imagery combinations pull in the best results, which email copy gets the most click-throughs.

What value goals could you set? Setting goals around the value you are going to add to the industry and to those in attendance at the Discovery Day gives you a deeper purpose than simply selling franchises. Visibility goals can really help you become clear on how you want to promote your brand. I include things like industry PR and podcast guest speaker interviews.

Set yourself or your team rewards for hitting each goal. If you were working in a sales team, there would be bonuses and incentives for achieving targets. Make this exercise enjoyable and fun, to motivate yourself to hit those targets.

Timelines

This is really the gold dust section of the launch plan. This is a replicable timeline for each Discovery Day to roll out time and time again, testing and measuring results and monitoring those metrics as you go each time.

Insert all the dates into the Gantt chart timeline and carry out the tasks associated. They are split into ones that can be automated or scheduled, and those you need to action on the day to make it super easy for you to implement.

Socials

Update your personal social media profiles with a cover picture that outlines the benefits of being a franchisee with your brand and "Click Here" for more details. Then add the information and link to your next Discovery Day in the description. When you are commenting on Facebook, anyone who clicks on your profile will be able to see clearly how they could get more information about your franchise offering.

Prepare the social posts detailed in the Gantt chart in advance and schedule them to go out. After you've prepared them once and done the work, you have them for every other Discovery Day you host until you want to tweak.

List all the different objections you have heard franchisees use as blocks to them coming on board, and next to each, note how you can overcome that objection for the right candidates.

21
AFTER YOUR DISCOVERY DAY

THERE ARE various different ways you can maximise brand exposure post discovery day. Holding a Discovery Day is a fantastic opportunity to get some PR. You can take photographs and do a write up for a press release. Send it out to industry press and franchise press too. With industry press releases, consider featuring a case study of someone who attended the Discovery Day so you are showing those potential franchisees available options. For example, "This is xx and they are currently doing xx and they are looking at xx because they would like a better work life balance which running xx would provide them with". You should always obtain permission from the person you are featuring, or make it anonymous. Follow some of the tips we looked at earlier to promote the results of your Discovery Day.

Follow up with everyone who attended the Discovery Day and take them to the next step, whether this is raising a deposit invoice or thanking them for their time and wishing them well for the future. Make sure each attendee feels valued as an individual, whether or not they choose to move forward with your franchise. Try to get feedback on why those who aren't moving forward don't feel it is the right fit for them, and use those reasons to objection handle at your next Discovery Day and on your social media platforms.

Prepare draft franchise agreements for those who are moving forward and map out their territories. Carry out a written or voice-recorded self-critique. Take the personal element out as best you can and pick apart the whole process you followed using the Gantt chart, including what you felt went well, what went terribly, and what you could improve on next time.

HOW TO CLOSE A FRANCHISE SALE

22

HOW THE PROSPECT FEELS

After going through the funnel and reaching the stage where you are looking to confirm a prospect or not, it is important to take into account their perspective. They are likely to be completely out of their comfort zone with butterflies in their tummies. Buying a franchise territory could mean leaving behind something they have spent years doing and training for, and the security blanket of a regular wage. This is massive for them! They may well be sweaty palmed and anxious.

Although in their heads, it may have seemed like a fabulous idea to come on board, actually committing to signing the Franchise Agreement and handing over thousands of pounds they may have saved hard for, can mean they resort to the fight, freeze, flight responses. Some will want to stay and fight for what they want and go for it. Others will be frozen like a deer in headlights, and then there will be those who take that flight option and back out at this late stage using any excuse they can. As frustrating as it is for the franchisor, it is understandable, and to be frank, better to find out now that they are not the right fit for the brand than further down the line when they are on board.

You will need to reassure them and paint a picture of what being a franchisee with your brand will be like. Give them confidence by showing them case studies and introduce them to other franchisees so they can have a chat without you present. Show them the pathway to coming onboard, always scheduling in the next step with them. Guide them through so they know where they are now, what the next step is, what the light at the end of the tunnel looks like, and when they will get there.

Set the dates for their training before they sign so it is in their diaries and they can start getting their heads around the fact this is real. Make sure the dates work for them. Demonstrate that signing the Franchise Agreement and paying their invoice is just another step in the process to running their own business and that you will lead them through each stage until they reach that point. Having reassurance that you are holding their hands already, just as you will do when they come on board, helps make it as seamless as possible for them.

23
HELPING THEM TO MAKE A DECISION

Help franchisees to make a decision about coming on board when you are sure they are the right fit for the brand. Ask them what they will do if they don't come on board. Will their life still be the same this time next year? There's a great saying by Henry Ford: "If you always do what you've always done, you'll always get what you've always got."

Show them what problems you can solve for them through your business model. You will have identified in your earlier calls why they are looking at buying a franchise. It may be because they want to be present for their family or because they are unhappy with their current position. Maybe they have elderly parents they want to be around for.

Demonstrate how running a franchise with you can help them with this.

Try and unpeel the layers of why they really want to come on board. What was the pivotal moment that made them take the steps to look at your option.? See if you can find out where they want to be in five years' time. If they don't know, add value and help them identify it, then include how running a franchise with you can support that five year vision.

Pay in to their emotional bank account and add heaps of value so that when you want to make a withdrawal by asking them to sign the Franchise Agreement, you have sufficiently paid in and built that "know, like, trust" to make it a straightforward decision for them.

Your language when you are closing a sale is really important. You are asking open questions or "this and that" questions. Asking questions that can be answered "yes" or "no" leads to dead ends. Build your prospects' confidence but also show confidence in your brand and your ability as a franchisor. Reassure them you have a support network behind you so they know that if anything happened to you, they and their investment would be protected.

Create a Frequently Asked Questions document or web page where you answer any common questions and objections, and use these to handle objections when closing sales. It may be you know that finance is a common concern, so perhaps you could partner with a lender or explain that you accept government-backed start-up loans. Don't be afraid to ask what is stopping them moving forward at that stage. Everyone has different personal circumstances and without asking about them, you don't know what's going on.

From your perspective, things may be going swimmingly. The Discovery Day has happened and prospects have submitted a fabulous business plan. You're looking to take a deposit and the Franchise Agreement has been prepared for signing. However, from their perspective they could be in the freeze or flight zone and they need extra support in their decision-making process. An open question like "Is there anything you can see as a barrier to you coming on board as a franchisee?" is invaluable. That said, don't be afraid to ask for the sale. "Are you ready for me to send you the invoice over?"

24
PARTNERING WITH LENDERS

PARTNERING with lenders can remove an obstacle to franchisees coming on board and add an extra layer of reassurance to prospective franchisees that these institutions are comfortable in the robustness of your business model. I partnered the first business I franchised with NatWest Bank, although most major banks have a franchising arm. Banks like the franchising industry because it is a proven business model they are lending against so a low risk for them in terms of recouping the monies lent. There are other options including government backed loans, angel investors, crowd funding and many more.

You must never be seen to be giving financial advice unless you are a financial advisor, as this will see you in breach of Financial Conduct Authority regulations. Make sure when speaking to potential franchisees about funding options you use appropriate wording and disclaimers to ensure you are on the right side of the law.

The process to get my business model approved by the bank was comprehensive. I needed to submit our Franchise Agreement, business plans, example cashflows for Head Office and for franchisees, and evidence that there was viability in the market place. The business model is the element being approved, rather than the individual. They have to undergo the usual checks that would be expected when applying for commercial finance. I was assigned a contact at the bank to refer prospects looking for funding too. I have found having the extra layer of checks the bank carries out was very reassuring as a franchisor.

25
YOUR TOOLKIT

YOUR "CLOSING A SALE" toolkit can differ depending on the brand and what you feel is right to include in your toolkit at any one time. I worked with Mr Action Coach, Brad Sugars himself for three days, and also one of his Action Coach franchisees when I was going through the pilot stage of franchising for the first time. Action Coach provided a money back guarantee on their initial franchise fee. I introduced this into Dog First Aid and guaranteed I would refund the initial fee and terminate the agreement if they were unable to make that money back in the first twelve months. The criteria to claim the initial franchise fee back was tight. For example, personal and professional growth is something that I'm passionate about.

You never stop learning, and from an accountability and motivation perspective, it is invaluable to keep your mind open through education. One of my criteria was to read and submit a review from my recommended reading list every month. Another was to submit a monthly self-critique of what they had done that month and what they felt went well, what could have been improved and how they would action this.

Guarantees aren't for all franchisors though. If the monies are going into the working capital of the business and you are not confident you will have the monies to refund, this might not be a good option for you. I was never in a position that saw me having to refund a franchise fee under the guarantee. However, offering this was effective for me. I was very confident in my business model and knew it worked well. It also gave me a get-out clause with franchisees that were underperforming and not accurately implementing the business model. After a year, I had the option to refund them and part ways with the Franchise Agreement.

Bundles are a great option to have in your toolkit. You could have a Silver, Gold, Platinum offering for your franchise, for example. I partnered with my business coach and, as part of the higher level bundle, the new franchisee received business coaching with my coach for three months. This demonstrated my commitment to the franchisee's ongoing success and the level of reinvestment into their future business growth. It doesn't have to be an external provider. It could be that you use equipment or marketing as a bundling tool. Maybe you have a social media package you can offer.

Discounts might also work for you. Personally, I prefer to add value rather than to discount. That said, for your pilot territories (the first 3-5 franchisees that come on board) you can offer a significant discount because you are going to be working closely with them to iron out any teething problems and creases in the model before rolling the model out nationally and potentially internationally in the future. The other problem I have with discounting initial franchise fees is that it potentially undervalues the individual franchisees' businesses for your existing franchisees. Say you have a franchisee who is building a franchise territory to sell for their retirement fund or a house deposit, and they have an end value in mind. Suddenly, it's announced by Head Office that they have slashed their initial fee by 50% and their asset has significantly diminished in value. By helping prospective franchisees to see the monetary value of the added element is more ethical in my mind.

Keep an open mind and don't assume anything at any stage of the sale process. Be open to communication and the thoughts and feelings of the potential franchisee at all times. However, do so in a way that protects your mindset by not oversharing personal matters, and likewise, try not to let them overshare personal matters with you either. Although you need a great relationship with your franchisees, oversharing personal information can blur the lines in a franchisor / franchisee relationship by becoming emotionally invested in each other's lives.

26
PRACTICAL STEPS

There are several practical steps that are handy to take to help with the closing of your franchise sales. Map out the territory that the prospective franchisee will be looking at in advance. It may be you've already got all of your territories mapped out, or perhaps you are mapping on a case-by-case basis. No two territories are identical and demographics can vary significantly. For example, a territory in central London would be miniscule in comparison to a territory with the same demographics in North Scotland. Considerations need to take into account the viability of such a vast area when increased travel time and costs need to be considered and how the knock on effect will impact cashflow forecasts.

Taking a deposit and asking the prospect to put their money where their mouth is sets a precedence for taking action and exchanging funds. Whether or not the deposit is refundable is down to the individual brand. You may choose to offer a percentage refund should the prospect not progress after seeing the Franchise Agreement, or to refund in full, or not at all. Whatever you decide should be transparent prior to the deposit being paid and potentially an "Intention to Proceed" document signed by the prospect. I would not send the draft Franchise Agreement without a deposit being taken as it is an expensive legal document designed to protect my brand. I feel it appropriate to see a level of commitment in return. That said, it can set warning bells off for the prospective franchisee as they are being asked to pay a deposit for something they haven't yet been able to see. It may be that you would feel comfortable showing a brief Heads of Terms of the Franchise Agreement along with perhaps the contents page of your Operations Manual if you have a prospect who is anxious at this stage.

As part of the financial information you discuss with the franchisee, include that they should budget to have the Franchise Agreement reviewed by a solicitor. I always recommend a handful of solicitors I have worked with and trust. If they go to Joe Bloggs High Street solicitor that deals with family law, you will likely end up with reems of questions because the solicitor is not familiar with franchising and doesn't necessarily understand the importance of having the Franchise Agreement weighted in the favour of the franchisor. A solicitor specialising in franchising will have a better understanding of everything involved.

If your franchisees are training under Limited companies, consider introducing your prospect to your accountant to support them through the set-up of their Limited company. Make sure your Franchise Agreement ties in them as an individual as well as their Limited company. If they are not personally tied in to the Agreement they could sell the shares out of the Limited company or strike it off meaning you are not able to hold the franchisee you recruited liable to the terms and conditions of the Franchise Agreement. You spend a lot of money and time as a franchisor getting to the point of making a sale, so make sure you have invested sufficiently in the legal documents to get this right.

Until the Franchise Agreement is signed and the money transferred, the deal is not done and the sale is not closed. Even after they have paid a deposit, I have had a prospective franchisee back out of the sale and take that flight option. You may get requests for payment instalments so the initial franchise fee can be spread over a certain time frame. I am wary of payment requests because they may come on board, see all of your brand secrets and then decide it's not for them. This opens a whole can of worms of unpleasantness to get the monies owed. If they are serious about running your franchise model in their area, they will source the initial franchise fee amount.

Finally, don't be disheartened if a franchisee you had your heart set on doesn't work out. Joanne Budden, owner of Leapfrog Sports had a disappointing experience with a potential franchisee. "She seemed the perfect fit all along, from the first call to travelling a distance to meet me and see the classes and discuss all the details at a Discovery Day. She was enthusiastic, had lots of plans and had already begun researching her local area for venues to hold the multi-sports classes we run.

Things were progressing well. Happily, she wanted to go ahead, and I felt she was a definite new franchisee who would be a success! However, shortly after receiving the Franchise Agreement, she started to question lots of what was included. This was no problem – it is important to understand fully what you are signing. I also always recommend seeking legal advice before signing. She then explained that she had a legal qualification herself (although was very vague on what that was) and began to negotiate the Franchise Agreement. She wanted me to amend it and make changes specific to her, adding in and removing clauses and reducing the fees paid to me."

Budden found things became uncomfortable during the negotiations, so she withdrew the offer of the franchise, which was "a disappointment but [she] knew deep down this was the right decision for [her] and the brand." Budden went on to find success with other franchisees, saying, "My first franchisee is doing even better than I hoped and has replaced her teaching salary in the first year of the franchise."

Another advocate for weathering the storms and persevering is Sarah Dalton, owner of The Baby Cloud. “I meticulously planned my pilot franchisee launch and recruited my very first franchisee last year. I made sure everything I could anticipate would be needed was in place. I am an "all my ducks in a row" kind of person.

The feedback from the recruitment and training was amazingly positive. The franchisee came on in leaps and bounds through the training and we both felt in a great place when it came to her launch. We had her three-month review recently and while the business hadn't grown quite as quickly as she’d anticipated, everything about the support system and programme had worked amazingly well for her.

At four months, this wonderful franchisee found out she was pregnant, which of course should always be celebrated. However, the pregnancy affected her health severely, almost immediately, meaning we had to very quickly make some decisions. Should I enforce the contract and ask that she take on an employee so early in her business? Or should we agree to mutually terminate the agreement so she could concentrate on her family and health without the pressure of a business? Of course, I opted for the second route. As a family focused business, I felt doing the right thing here was most important. After six months of nurturing this franchisee (the first six months being the most intense) of course I was absolutely gutted to lose this 'investment', but I believe everything happens for a reason. I signed my next two franchisees within one month of this happening, so I was onwards and upwards."

FRANCHISOR SALES MINDSET

I believe that because my mindset was not in the right place when I launched my franchise offering for the first time, it stopped me from actually selling pilot territories. I had to do some mental decluttering and work on my own mindset before I was able to propel the franchise forward.

A lot of people don't like sales because they associate it with being sleazy or hard-selling – perhaps used car salesmen or dodgy telesales reps ringing and ringing. Full disclosure: my first job entailed selling double glazing over the phone and I have been selling my whole life. With every business I've started, I have been the sales team in the beginning because there was no one else to do it. I imagine you were the same when you started your business. It's really important that you think like a sales rep if you are to employ one. As the founder of the business though, you have the passion and drive to sell because you know the difference your products and/or services make to the end user. It's why you started the business in the first place. So, let's get that mindset in the right place so you can sell more franchises.

27
IMPOSTER SYNDROME

Franchisor imposter syndrome is rife. It is never more prevalent than in those initial stages of being a franchisor. You've franchised your business and been working your butt off to bring your franchise to the market, but suddenly you've gone from selling something that is a few pounds, to something that is thousands of pounds. You may get all sorts of doubts creeping in and you may feel like a fraud. You're telling people that you have franchised, but don't actually have any franchisees on board. It's a very strange time in a franchisor's lifecycle. Further down the line when you've got franchisees on board, that imposter syndrome creeps in again and you're faced with different challenges. You're faced with new situations at every stage of your franchising journey that can test you. I like to think of them as learning opportunities that help me to grow.

Imposter syndrome is when you feel like you're not good enough. You can be so far out of your comfort zone that you doubt yourself and your business. You may wonder whether you should be on this road at all. I remember the first time I stood up at a networking event to do my elevator pitch and said, "My name's Jo Middleton and I am the franchisor of Dog First Aid. I help veterinary professionals and dog lovers run their own business with my proven successful business model, so that they can choose their own working hours and income levels whilst being their own boss for themselves but not by themselves." I felt like such a fraud! It was super uncomfortable. I was sweating and my knees were shaking. But the more I did it and the more I was able to see the benefits I was offering people by bringing them on board as franchisees, the easier it became.

Have you ever heard the term "monkey chatter"? Or "mind monkeys"? They're those little voices that creep into your head saying things like, "Who are you to do that?" "No one will be interested in it." "It will never succeed anyway." "Your franchisees will never like it." "Franchisees don't like change, so you can't do that," blah blah blah! I've learned a few different ways to manage these thoughts.

Method 1

Firstly, recognise that it is just that – mind monkey chatter. It's your mind's natural way of trying to protect you from doing something that could be a risk and is outside of your comfort zone. Secondly, acknowledge it and thank your brain for trying to protect you and keep you safe. Then, try visualising the monkey sitting in front of you, pull out a banana gun and blast it away with banana custard. I'm not sure of the psychological evidence behind this, as it sounds ridiculous, but it works for me.

Method 2

Stick your thumb out in front of you with a straight arm – a bit like a thumbs up. Have your thumb speak the internal dialogue back to you in a silly small voice. "You're not good enough," "Who are you to be a franchisor?" "You haven't sold a territory in ages, no one is going to buy one now."

Whatever those mind monkeys are, have them talk back to you in a silly little voice from your thumb. This method featured in one of the first self-help books I ever read back in 2007 – *Change Your Life in Seven Days* by Paul McKenna. Although it didn't change my life in the seven days I read it, I truly believe that it changed my life.

Imagine someone you love dearly. Now picture someone saying all the things your mind monkeys say to you, to them. Would you ever let someone speak to them like that? No! Absolutely not. You'd stick up for them. So stick up for yourself and don't let your mind monkeys bully you.

You need to think like the epic business owner that you are, and make decisions accordingly. Knowing the value of your franchise offering will naturally help. I don't mean the financial value but the value it will bring to peoples' lives. You are transforming them from where they are now, to where they want to be.

Another way to help overcome imposter syndrome is to learn some statistics off by heart about the industry your business operates in and the franchise industry too. These facts and statistics support why your business model works. It gives you confidence because of the third party validation that there is a need for the offering. I write these down on post-it notes and place them in random spots around the house and office so they sink into my subconscious throughout my everyday life.

Don't get things perfect, get them done. Yes, of course you should proofread something and do due diligence appropriately before taking action, however, if this turns into procrastination it allows more time for those mind monkeys to creep in.

28
GOOD HABITS

Franchisor sales mindset is a constant work in progress. Getting into good habits helps you get back onto the sales mindset train. Leading your franchisees by example and consistently focusing on your personal and professional development will reap benefits for your brand longer term.

Studies have shown that if you do something consistently for 28 days, it becomes a habit. I don't think I've ever stuck to something daily for 28 days for it to become a habit, so I can't say that is right or not. For me, it's a conscious process of having tasks and calendar reminders. I have Monday Marketing and Finance Friday, for example. If I find I've slipped in an area, I make a calendar appointment with myself as if it's a meeting that can't be missed. I take myself off to a nearby hotel and order a hot drink before switching my phone off and plugging in my noise-cancelling headphones. I don't leave until I've done what needs doing. I then rinse and repeat until it's a habit again.

I'll tell you more about some of the good habits that have been transformational to me below, but I want to be vulnerable in this book and share why they were so important. Just as I went through the franchising process for the first time and had the franchise website built, my dad was given six weeks to live. He'd told me it was a year but his palliative care nurse broke it to me that it was six weeks. It was a lot to get my head around. The Operations Manual had been written, the Franchise Agreement drafted and everything was all prepared. I passed everything over to my AWESOME virtual assistant, Stefanie Cowles. Stefanie dealt with everything for a few months and I will be forever grateful to her for her support at that time. She tested all the systems and processes that were laid out in the Operations Manual, because she was running the business.

When I came back, I was hollow, and quite frankly rather traumatised. Anyone who has lost a parent and watched their health decline in that way may be able to relate. In my head, I somehow related the franchise business with my father dying. This may sound strange but the website was one of the last things I showed him before he was too ill to understand any more. I couldn't recognise it at the time. I got hundreds of enquiries but wasn't following things up properly. They maybe had one auto email and that was it. My sales process and my sales mindset were absolutely not in alignment.

So, I implemented these good habits and they helped to snap me out of my hollow, grieving mindset and get my head in the game. I can't stress how important they are. If they were able to help me get from where I was to building the franchise business up to be valued at six figures in a short space of time, then I truly believe they can help you too.

A.B.C.

This stands for Always Be Connecting, although I have also heard it used as Always Be Calling in the sales world. As I've already mentioned, building a warm audience to sell to is key. Part of this is consistently connecting with your ideal franchisees. You need to implement the 4 P's to profile them, so you know who they are and where to find them first. I have a calendar reminder on LinkedIn at 8 a.m. every morning to connect with ten new people. At the time of writing, LinkedIn doesn't like users to add more than ten new connections a day and can restrict people if they do more.

For me, my ideal franchisees for Wizziwoos Kids Clubs are on LinkedIn so that's where I focus. If your ideal franchisees are predominantly on a different social media platform, connect with them there instead. Pop them a little message along the lines of "Hi, I love connecting with new people on here. I help (insert brand transformation statement). Hope you have a great day!" You're not selling anything, but simply connecting and being in their space. That way, when you do start putting content out that speaks to them as your ideal franchisees, they are more likely to read it and gravitate towards it. All you are doing is warming an audience up. This can take up to twelve months to do properly, so the sooner you hone that ideal franchisee profile and start connecting with them, the better.

Systemising and processing

As franchisors, we systemise and process every area of our business for our franchisees to follow. I would encourage you to have a Head Office Operations Manual where you have all the most current HQ systems and processes recorded. I don't mean spend the next six months doing this and letting it detract from your sales processes. Do it as you go along. It might be that you have something like GDrive or Dropbox that you can access from any device, and as you're carrying out a task, scribble down a flowchart of the process, take a picture and upload it or alternatively edit the relevant document in the cloud to note it down. Inject your personality, or the personality of your brand if it's different, into everything. That way, when the time comes to hand the systems and processes for the HQ franchise business over to a team member to free your time up, there is continuity and flow to keep that brand look and feel. When I talk about documenting everything, it includes not just the sales process but the franchisee training, onboarding, ongoing support, recruitment funnel and implementation.

Ultimately, you are building your franchise as an asset that has a resale value. Whether you choose to cash it in at any point is up to you, however, by building it in this way you are able to stop firefighting, think more strategically, and grow it with purpose and clarity.

This helps with your sales mindset because everything is being systemised and processed in line with your bigger picture goals. All areas of the business simply become processes for you to have fun with, rather than a daunting task. You can clearly assess which tasks don't bring you joy and put measures in place to outsource them first, knowing that because you have systemised and processed with personality, you are able to delegate confidently.

Automation

Try to be like a little sponge when it comes to technology platforms and software, even if they make you want to curl up in the corner and have a nap. We are living in a digital age and the more progressive we can be with technology, the faster we can grow. Automation is a fabulous tool when correctly set up to ensure that the "human" isn't lost in the system. Each person still needs to feel valued as an individual rather than just another number in your database. To do this you might insert a field to personalise an automated email and format it as plain text rather than HTML with funky pictures and graphics for example. I'm not saying you shouldn't make your newsletters pretty, but consider how it might make your prospects feel if they are always receiving communications that appear to be "salesy" rather than ones that speak to them directly.

Injecting your personality into the communication is key. This will stand you apart from competing brands that your prospect may also be looking at. They need to be able to see your passion, enthusiasm and energy when speaking to them. People buy from people that they know, like and trust. If they are simply getting a formal, boring, corporate piece of communication, they may switch off. Compare a franchisee support request auto responder that says "Thank you for your support request. We will contact you within 48 hours," with "I am so pleased to hear from you Rachel! I have logged your support request on the system and will get back to you by Friday. If it's a super urgent one then maybe you could post in the franchisee Facebook/WhatsApp group and one of the other franchisees might be able to help. I'm really looking forward to catching up with you though. Hope you have a great day."

Automate as much as you can and as far as you can but bear in mind you need to have a system that includes an element of human in it, but that you can also automate in some ways too.

Practise makes perfect

For me, practising things definitely makes a massive difference to my confidence when selling. For example I write facts and stats down on cue cards and repeat them as if I'm revising for an exam. Another lesson Brad Sugars, founder and franchisor of global franchise Action Coach, taught me was to make a list of "I am" statements. These are positive affirmations relating to the person you want to be and the things you want to achieve e.g. I am a successful franchisor, I am a magnet for the right franchisees for my brand, I am ambitious and driven to leave a positive legacy.

When you have your list, record them aloud and listen to them while you are going about your daily life. Perhaps while you are walking the dog, cooking or going for a run. That level of repetition on a regular basis is super powerful in programming your Reticular Activating System (RAS). It might be that you do this with testimonials you've received, your brand transformation statement or a 60 second elevator pitch. Maybe you know, or can gather, statistics about your franchisee network. For example, perhaps 65% of your franchisees added the additional revenue stream that you introduced six months ago and brought in a quarter more in revenue than the 35% that didn't. Speaking to yourself in the mirror or even just out loud while you're driving can also help.

Get in the zone and say cheese

Before I go live on camera, I have a little routine to get myself in the zone and raise my energy levels. I do ten star jumps, carry out some vocal exercises and smile for three minutes. It lifts me and removes the "stuff" that is going on around me during the rest of the day and gets me in the zone. Have a think about how you can lift your energy levels in certain situations where you're going to need to be on your A game. What works for you? Might it be breath work or carrying out some emotional freedom technique? Maybe it's meditating. These all have a place in my life but I've found the star jumps, vocal exercises and smiling makes up the combination that raises my vibration.

29
ADAPTING QUICKLY

As franchisors we have so many decisions to make. Being able to make informed decisions quickly is a good skill to develop as your franchise network grows. Knowing your business numbers is really helpful as it enables you to make informed decisions and adapt to situations quickly. This was a real weak spot for me when I first started out in business. I ended up writing KYBN in different colours on A4 paper and sticking it all over my walls. KYBN stands for Know Your Bloody Numbers!

As businesses grow and you go down the franchising route, your numbers are really key to the ongoing success of the brand. You're selling territories based on demographics and financials that have already been achieved and proven as possible. You, of course, should never promise any revenue levels to a prospective franchisee, but you can most certainly demonstrate what is possible. If you don't know your numbers, how are you going to ethically sell franchise territories?

Don't promise a franchisee revenue. There are too many external factors are outside of your control. However, to be able to sleep at night, you need to know yourself that the territory you are selling them is viable based on track record.

The habits that have really benefited me are putting systems in place to measure, and read them weekly or monthly:

- Franchisee profit and loss reports
- Franchisee lead generation figures
- Franchisee cost of acquisition per customer
- Head Office profit and loss reports
- Head Office aged debtor and creditor reports
- Head Office balance sheet

And, of course, it's useful to know cash flow forecasts for both franchisor and franchisee businesses and compare them to the actual figures being achieved.

As the Head Office business grows, weekly number crunching is invaluable for keeping a focus on the figures. My way of keeping myself accountable is by getting my bookkeeper to email me the reports out weekly so that I review them.

Always have your franchisee systems set up so that you know their numbers and are able to make informed decisions quickly. Those informed decisions need to filter down to every area of the Head Office business. For example, if you know the numbers behind the marketing that you're doing, you can measure what is and isn't working. There is usually an 80/20 split, as in Pareto's Principle. Pareto's Principle refers to a typical distribution of 80% of results coming from 20% of actions. When you measure the numbers behind the advertising, it's really interesting to see how accurate this actually can be, with 80% of your leads coming from 20% of your marketing sources, for example. When armed with the numbers, you can make informed decisions and do more of the 20% that works, dramatically increasing your results. This strategic monitoring of numbers means that as the environment around you and your ideal franchisees changes, you are able to constantly and consistently tweak things so you are always on the front foot.

Use current situations to make informed decisions too. If someone achieves something in your network, test and measure it in a couple of different territories and see whether it works there too before rolling it out across the network enabling all franchisees to benefit. This in turn benefits the Head Office business in brand growth and usually increased royalties. Likewise, if there is an area that isn't working so well in your model, tweak it as soon as possible. Your franchisees are ultimately your customers, and while you'll never please all the people all the time, their support and input is valuable and important.

It is helpful to gather testimonials to boost recruitment. However, don't wait until your franchisee is successfully trading to do this. Ask for testimonials at each stage of their journey so that franchisees who are one step behind them can see what's possible. A great example of this is getting testimonials from franchisees when they have just come on board and finished their initial training before they start trading. The testimonials you gather about how supportive and comprehensive the training process was will inspire prospective franchisees to take the leap and sign on the dotted line. They can clearly see from these validations that you will deliver what you are promising. As well as asking questions on your feedback forms around how things can be improved, ask questions that will lead to testimonial-worthy answers, for example, 'The three things I have enjoyed most about the training are ____________.' If someone gives you a cracking answer, ask them to jump on a video and tell it to the camera, so you can use video testimonials as well as creating memes. At your annual conference, you can also get a photographer and videographer in to take professional photos and get video testimonials from your franchisees. If budgets are tight, consider contacting your local university or college and see if any students need work experience as part of their course.

Another way to benefit from adapting quickly is to keep an eye on the news and jump on anything you have an expert opinion about. At the time of writing we are, according to the media, in a time of economic downturn. This is relevant for you as a franchisor, and not necessarily in a negative way. Prospective franchisees are looking to buy into a franchise because it is a lower risk model than flying solo. This would be a perfect time to distribute a press release to all the industry publications your ideal franchisees may read. This means the industry they work in before they come on board with your franchise. If you're ever stuck, Twitter is a great place to search #journorequests and find journalists who are looking for comments about various topics.

30
FRANCHISOR SALES MINDSET HACKS

We've looked at ways to increase the value you're adding, and how you can strategically think about selling, rather than becoming side-tracked by imposter syndrome mind monkey chatter. To that end, here are some hacks to help you:

Know that your offering helps, and know who it helps

The ripple effect you are creating through your franchise business helps so many people. If you haven't got any franchisees yet, you're in a great place to do this exercise because you can start with a blank canvas and an idea of how many end users you can help. If you're already a franchisor with franchisees, you'll be able to calculate exactly how many people each franchisee is helping in their area. Your franchise will help the franchisees to choose their working hours, run their own business, have an asset they are building to sell on. In turn those franchisees will help their customers, the franchisees families and friends, the customers families and friends, the local communities too. The list of who is helped through your franchise goes on and on. All because of you! You deserve to be super confident! You need to be on a mission to help as many people as you can because of the massive ripple effect your awesome franchise has.

Mind your own business

Keep an eye on the competition and the market place, but mind your own business – look after you own business. Nurture it's development, focus on being innovative and forward thinking and making sure your franchisees are supported. It's easy to get caught up in what other people are doing in their businesses and not be laser-focused on your own. If you allow yourself to be distracted, you put yourself at risk of imposter syndrome and self-doubt kicking in. Use competition to fuel your own actions rather than using it as a stick to beat yourself with.

Make informed franchisee-centric decisions

Keeping your decisions franchisee-centred means you will always be progressing. Your franchisees need to be able to see positive actions being taken to grow the brand they have invested in to. However, some franchisees may be resistant to change. Make sure you keep communication lines open with your network and make decisions based on the franchisees' and brand growth. This will help you create a power team of franchisees who are all ambassadors for your brand.

Really listen

Practise active listening with your franchisees. It is easy to try and provide them with solutions all the time. However, actively listening by paying attention when they're talking, providing feedback and reflecting on what they've said before responding can help you to build trust and healthy franchisor/franchisee relationships.

Be uber helpful

You want to add value where possible to your network of franchisees. Whether it's a new leaflet design, a new social media asset or a new video they can use in their marketing that drips out once a month to the network, or you increase the frequency, it will make a difference to how they rate your brand. Listen to what they want and provide them with it where possible.

Pay into emotional bank accounts

In Stephen Covey's book *The 7 Habits of Highly Effective People*, he describes how you can imagine that everyone has an invisible emotional bank account. You pay into a person's emotional bank account through kindness, courtesy and by adding value to them. You can't make a withdrawal from the bank account until you've paid into it and built up enough reserves to do so. Think about how that might apply to your franchise leads. When someone expresses interest in your offering, how can you pay into their emotional bank account before you ask for the sale? Listen to their 'why' for coming on board and take note of the feelings that have led them to the decision of making a big and brave life change.

Calculate income per lead

If you know your numbers and conversion rates, you'll know that, for example, out of every 100 enquiries you will get one new franchisee. If your offering is £10,000 for example, for every lead you call back, you are banking £100. It makes following up enquiries and getting 99 no's so much easier if you switch your mindset to knowing that each time you pick up the phone or send a message and get ghosted, you still earned £100.

31

PEOPLE

Work with amazing people who are in line with your values. It will help eliminate any negative mind monkey chatter and help you make confident decisions quickly. It may be that you have an accountant who isn't proactive with their advice or doesn't answer your questions clearly. If that's the case, change them. This is your business and your rules. Anyone who comes into contact with your business needs to be the right fit and lift the vibration of your brand positively. By doing this, you are able to boost your mindset daily as you are having positive interactions all the time. Family and friends can, with the best of intentions, be absolutely crushing. So, think before you speak about your franchise. Some people will project their own mind monkeys, money mindset fears and opinions onto you when you don't need to hear it. If they haven't been there and done it, or they haven't actually walked the walk and are just talking the talk, and they aren't adding value, it can damage your mindset. You are being brave and bold to put yourself out there as a franchisor. Don't let negative nelly's get in your way. Smile and wave.

Join a peer support network and surround yourself both online and offline with awesome peers. A small note of caution though... Because franchising is associated by some with large amounts of money, it can be seen as a place where there is big money to be made. The reality is that, in the early days, after paying a consultant thousands of pounds and not having enough franchise fees to take a salary yourself, while desperately trying to recruit more franchisees, there is not an infinite money pot. However, there are some people who will try to schmooze you and tell you what you want to hear, while getting money from you. Being part of a peer support network that genuinely has your best interests at heart and wants to see you succeed is invaluable.

Sarah Mollison, owner of CYCLEme TOTS, agrees that having the right mindset and working with the right people can mean the difference between making your franchise business a success or something that can compound your self-belief:

"My biggest franchisee recruitment learning to date is that I am the best person to be in charge of that process in my business. I had some real mindset issues when it came to franchisee recruitment, and working with Jo helped give me confidence in my own abilities.

When we started the process to franchise our business I knew absolutely nothing about franchising and so we worked closely with BFA recommended franchise consultants to develop, optimise and then launch our franchise opportunity. It was a costly process and while they were great at getting our franchise opportunity to market, at every step of the journey I felt massively out of my depth with no real knowledge of how I was going to recruit a franchisee.

Furthermore, I did not have any friends or close connections who had previously franchised a business, so I was completely unaware of the typical lead conversion ratios for franchise sales.

Rather than looking at the bigger picture and believing that each of these enquiries was bringing me closer to my ideal franchisee, I convinced myself I was doing something wrong, which made me avoid contact or delay my follow up process – which of course resulted in fewer conversions and more self-doubt.

For a franchisor/franchisee relationship to work well, there has to be good communication from both sides, as well as trust and an alignment in the business direction and mission. Therefore, in order to ensure you are taking on the right franchisees for your brand, I highly recommend that you are the person having the initial conversations with prospective franchisees to make sure they are the right fit for your business."

Finally, on this subject of people, I want to mention the most important person... you! Back yourself, be yourself. You are enough. You have got this. You can do it. You have worked really hard to get to this point. Don't second guess yourself. You are awesome. I believe in you, so believe in yourself too.

32
HEAD OFFICE PROCESSES

Your franchisor sales mindset is going to be boosted by knowing that everything is covered and there is a system and process in place for each area of the Head Office business. Build an HQ Operations Manual. Think about the longer term and how you could remove yourself from the business eventually. If you were to hand over a document to someone else, could they pick it up and run your franchise, develop it, look for opportunities and build it towards your bigger picture vision? You've written an Operations Manual already and systemised and processed every area of the business for franchisees. Now you are running a different business. You are running the franchise Head Office business and I'd recommend going through the same process of writing an Operations Manual for this business too. What areas need your input and what can be outsourced? Reminder, delegate don't abdicate. Stamp your personality on everything – you are a massive part of the brands USP.

An area you need to examine as you systemise your Head Office business is time investment. The time invested is currently yours. You love your business and probably put way more time and energy into it than any employee might. But, imagine if it was costing you £40/hour to pay someone to do the work you're doing. You want the time investment to be streamlined where possible. Batching tasks can be really help with this, as can using technology to automate tasks where possible, while injecting personality where possible. Block out time to respond to enquiries, to check your emails, and to go on social media, so there is structure and routine rather than chaos and disorganisation. Also block out pockets of time for you to switch off and process – free time. Maybe go for a walk or a swim or binge watch a film in your pj's with a takeaway. This "brain switch-off time" is often where the best ideas come out. You may also be more productive after a break. When you are constantly on the go, you are regularly functioning from adrenalin rather than from a logical strategic place of calm.

ONBOARDING NEW FRANCHISES

If you get the onboarding stage right you set the foundations for a long term, fruitful relationship for both you and the franchisee, and they will become independent sales reps for your brand without even realising it. People buy from recommendations and if you set your franchisees up properly during the onboarding process, you plant the seeds for future franchisee recruitment through their own word of mouth. You're also paying into those emotional bank accounts and continuing to build on that "know, like, trust" with them. However, what we commonly see in the industry is that when a new franchisee comes on board, they are super excited and bursting at the seams with enthusiasm. But then just three months down the line they start to become a little disheartened with the challenges that crop up or the hard work needed to get more customers begins. The dip in energy needs to be predicted and allowed for in your onboarding system so there is something happening to lift them and keep them motivated around that time.

33
NEW FRANCHISEE MINDSET

In a new franchisee's head, they have just transferred a big lump sum of their money to you, or got themselves into a substantial amount of debt. They want to know that the money is an investment rather than being flushed down the toilet. They need to see how they can make that money back, and how and when they will get a return on their investment. With every new business, money isn't going to come straight in and it's important you don't imply that in the sales process. Demonstrating during the onboarding process that all the numbers are achievable and working with franchisees to set the targets they need to reach to get that return on investment is really valuable. Find out how they like to be held accountable, how they can be motivated, and what incentives they could put in place to help them stay on track. They may have "helpful" family and friends who have given inaccurate information because they don't understand the franchise business model or see the value in handing over a lump sum to a franchisor rather than setting up a business and flying solo. Your new franchisee may have been subjected to unhelpful comments about "throwing their money down the pan", making them believe they've been ripped off. So, not only have they got their own mind monkeys, but they've got other people projecting theirs onto them too. You can relate, right?. It's therefore really important to evidence to your new franchisees that you know what you're doing, there is a proven system and process in place, and there's an underpinning current of support for them to tap in to whenever they need it.

During the initial onboarding process, you are showing new franchisees the path. As with every step we go through from the top of the funnel through to growing their franchise business, you are showing them the next steps. They will be able to sleep at night knowing they are in safe hands.

Encourage franchisees to leave all their knowledge at the door and start afresh and trust the process. Show them you've got this covered. All they need to do is pick up the tools you've provided them with and use them according to the instructions you've given them.

34
THE ONBOARDING PROCESS

THE PROCESS of onboarding a new franchisee needs to be systemised and processed too. Just like every other area of the business, you need to have a *franchisor* Head Office system and process, and a *franchisee* system and process. Every area between them signing the Agreement and being customer-facing needs to be written out and processed, whether it's the equipment to be ordered, or the marketing launch.

Key documents like the Operations Manual, training log and brand stock imagery can be sent automatically using a drip campaign. When franchisees first come on board, send them a link every day to something new to read or use. The first day should focus on the pathway and showing franchisees exactly what will be happening during their first few weeks, including any key dates they need to be aware of and actions they need to take. For example, do they need to get a new mobile number for their business and email it to you, so you can generate their marketing materials?

Just a side note on having additional manuals outside of the Operations Manual. I have seen many brands use additional manuals such as a Brand Guidelines Manual, Territory Resale Manual, and Brand Social Media Guidelines Manual. The Franchise Agreement does not refer to the these manuals but only to the Operations Manual. It may be that your Franchise Agreement does not tie these in legally and it only requires the franchisee to comply with the Operations Manual. If in doubt speak, to your franchise solicitor so they can ensure your franchisees are tied into the full organisational guidance you lay out. Alternatively, include them all as part of your Operations Manual.

Have everything laid out in an easy to follow way. You may have use a project management tool like Asana or Trello or perhaps a good old spreadsheet with an onboarding timeline. This way you can roll it out easily time and time again, and make occasional changes.

If you have in-person or live virtual franchisee training, schedule the dates before the franchisee signs the Franchise Agreement, to help them over the line in a timely manner. Until the Agreement is signed, it's not a done deal. By having the training dates scheduled, you are showing them the next step in the pathway and how you will be setting them up for success.

Every franchisee that comes on board will help shape the future onboarding system and process. You'll receive feedback through the onboarding as different franchisees come from different backgrounds, have different experiences and learn in different ways. Use this feedback to hone your materials and delivery accordingly.

35
LAUNCH

THE FIRST DAY of business can see franchisees quaking in their boots with big butterflies in their tummies. I once went out and shadowed a new franchisee delivering her first Dog First Aid course and she was physically shaking and drinking Rescue Remedy like there was no tomorrow. I recognised that the pre-launch support needed to include more work around confidence and self-worth. I incorporated an element of "dummy run" to the process where franchisees set up their equipment (projector/laptop/screen etc) and recorded themselves delivering the course to a screen / phone camera. They also carried out a self-critique and submitted the recording to Head Office. This helped us see whether they were ready to go live in front of customers or needed further support . It also meant they were able to take stock of how much they actually knew, and appreciate how far they had come since joining, while also identifying any areas they still wanted to work on without the pressure of getting it wrong. Giving your franchisees constructive feedback while empowering them helps them increase their revenue while building their confidence in running their own business with your brand.

During your initial training sessions, it is helpful to have several new franchisees starting out at the same time. It creates more of a buzz, feels less intense and encourages people to bounce off each other. Everyone brings new ideas to the table and the excitement for their new venture is infectious. They get to speak to other franchisees who are in the same position and it reinforces their decision to come on board, because others have too. Different franchisees will ask different questions that others might not have thought of which helps them get the most out of the sessions.

It's great to have existing franchisees share their experiences, tips and stories while you are training new franchisees, so that they have something to aspire to. At their launch try to have a Head Office team member or another franchisee there to support them. It's important to stress it's a cheerleader to support them rather than to judge. They need to know it's okay to make mistakes. We are all human and all make mistakes, particularly when finding our feet. Only the franchisee and the Head Office team member / other franchisee will likely know that they have made the mistake – the customer is unlikely to realise. The franchisee will get a big sinking feeling. It can put them off their stride and make the rest of their day feel like it has gone downhill, but mistakes are simply a part of learning. Once open for business, your franchisees will need to self-evaluate to aid their continued growth and development. What went really well in that session? What could have gone better? What feedback did the customer give?

36
ONGOING SUPPORT

START to wean franchisees off your close support after they have proved they are competent. Head Office needs to be a resource rather than a prop. At the initial training, discuss the level of ongoing support the franchisee can expect. This might include weekly support calls for the first couple of months, then changing to bi-weekly before becoming monthly and eventually ending up as quarterly review meetings. Let them know if you have a support ticket system to raise queries on, or whether they will have unlimited support by email. Set their expectations regarding response times then try to exceed them with outstanding customer service. Stress that they will find most of the answers to their questions in the Operations

Manual, and show them how to search the document for key words if possible. And, of course, make sure the levels of support you provide are laid out in the Operations Manual.

Many years ago, I had a boss who told me that when I was managing my team I needed to hold their hands, not wipe their bottoms. It is the same with franchisees. Hand-hold and support them, be there to guide them and show them how they can move their businesses forward, but don't do everything for them. You need to empower them to be successful and stand on their own two feet running the business within the parameters of the model.

In order to grow your Head Office business, you have to have the time to focus on strategy. Until you reach around ten franchisees, your network may have a really cool family feel, but this can considerably blur the lines if you're not careful. There's nothing wrong with being friendly with your franchisees at all. However, if you are seen as more of a mate than the franchisor, franchisees can become disgruntled when you need to delegate support to a franchise development manager or similar. You physically can't provide the same level of support to twenty franchisees as you did when there were only three. This is another reason why you should know what your brand will look like long term. You can then start planting the seeds for this through the onboarding process, so franchisees know what to expect.

If you are at the piloting stage, it is of course important to work closely with franchisees so you can iron out any creases in the Operations Manual. They have come on board at a discounted rate to help you with this. You can lay out the expectations of what support will look like and how for a certain time period that support will work both ways. You are going to be feeding back to them on their performance, and helping them grow a successful business, and they are going to feed back to you about your Operations Manual and systems. Let them know that the bigger the brand grows, the more their territory will be worth further down the line, so they can see the ongoing value. Set their expectations for how long the two-way support will last, and what their support will look like from that point on, so they don't expect more.

Communication is key. It can be tricky to please the whole network, but maintaining good relationships where possible will save you a heap of sleepless nights and grey hairs. Assess the ongoing support process as you craft it, particularly in the early stages, to make sure it provides the franchisees with the value and support they need.

Motivation and accountability are two key factors to consider. Thinking strategically about how you can inject fun into all areas of being a franchisee under your brand. When franchisees are having fun they stay motivated, and they don't mind you holding them accountable to their goals. Some franchisees want to stay on more regular support calls so they can be held accountable for achieving their goals. Fun also helps with the continued trust in the franchisor/franchisee relationship and the paying into their emotional bank accounts. They can see that your interest isn't only in their KPI's and their franchise fees but also with their overall happiness. The fun then trickles down to their customers and leaves a positive taste in the mouths of everyone who comes in to contact with the brand.

Once you have an established network, you can have a buddy system where franchisees can touch base with someone in the same boat or has been there and done it. It means they can see things from a different angle, and it also takes the pressure off you a bit. You may also find that when they are having frank conversations with a peer rather than you as the franchisor, things come out that may not otherwise be brought to your attention. These areas can then be tweaked if appropriate.

Don't take feedback or complaints personally. I know that seems easy to say when actually it can feel really personal. You've put in hard graft and burned the midnight oil to get the systems and processes right. It can feel like a personal attack when you have a franchisee who is not happy and makes sure you are fully aware of their feelings about it. You need to practise what you preach and take it as a learning experience. Don't get defensive. Take some time for self-care and reflection, then come back stronger. There will always be critique on the areas you have laid out, as having a franchise is a constantly evolving process. It needs to be to keep things fresh and improving all the time.

During the initial training, you need to also make it clear to franchisees that the Operations Manual will be, periodically and fairly regularly at times, amended. Let them know how they will be notified of these amendments. Some franchisees in your network will be opposed to change and struggle with this so it is better to set these expectations right at the beginning of their journey. Explain that the Manual needs to be updated to ensure the network has access to current guidelines and shared best practices. You want to keep innovating, keep the brand fresh and current, and that change needs to be embraced rather than pushed against. Of course, there will be times when you are the big bad wolf, however, I think it is fairer for franchisees and easier for you to be transparent about this during the onboarding process.

Julie Barber, owner of TechyTots Ltd found that providing support when times were particularly challenging paid off: "One of our franchisees experienced a slow start returning after the pandemic. They were worried about the ability of their business to recover. To support them, we provided lots of training and developed a plan to assist them in resuming classes and expanding their reach. With our support and motivation, the franchisee was able to implement the plan successfully and is now running more classes than before. They have even hired a new staff member to help run the additional classes. In fact, they are in the process of recruiting more staff to expand their reach and further grow their business. By providing our franchisees with the necessary resources, training, and guidance, we were able to help them navigate a difficult period and achieve success. Our partnership with them demonstrates the importance of supporting and empowering franchisees to overcome challenges and achieve their goals."

37
EVALUATION

This section is all about you carrying out your own evaluation of the onboarding process. Let's start by looking at the numbers. Remember KYBN? Know exactly how much you need to spend to recruit each new franchisee. Put an amount in for the time commitment for the onboarding process too. How much time did you or a member of your team need to spend on onboarding the new franchisee and how much did that cost you? If it's your time spent decide on your hourly rate and use it to calculate. Figure out as accurate a cost of acquisition per franchisee as possible. Don't forget to include your marketing spend in that too. Calculate your net profit margin and then decide how much of the net profit per franchisee onboarded is going to be reinvested into marketing for the next franchisees who come onboard. Use these numbers to forecast cashflow and play with the numbers to see what would need to happen financially to achieve your franchisee recruitment goals.

Revisit any previous goals that you've set (whether they are on the back of a napkin or not) and set new ones. Carry out a self-critique of what went well and what didn't during the onboarding and training process. What could have gone better and how could it have been improved? What did you find clunky and what wasn't "clean" in the process? What did franchisees write on their feedback forms at the sessions?

It might be that you found the process zapped all your energy and you needed a week to recover from the onboarding and training sessions. If you identify that, you can then factor it in next time you recruit, so you can diarise a week of downtime after new franchisee onboarding. You'll have identified a need and put systems in place to ensure that all social media is scheduled to go out and any other things that need to happen in your absence. You can then take the time you need to recharge your batteries without worrying.

Tweak everything that needs to be tweaked and then rinse and repeat and recruit more franchisees.

38
FINAL WORDS

As Karen Gibb of Mind Marvels put it so well, being a franchisor is not for the faint hearted! In her words: “It's a constant sales funnel to find the right people, train them up, and support them in running a profitable business. But despite the challenges, I wouldn't trade it for anything in the world.”

She goes on to say: “One of the things I love most about franchising is the opportunity to help others achieve their dreams. I remember when I first started out with Mind Marvels, I was just a single location trying to make a difference in the lives of children. But now, through franchising, I'm able to spread that impact far and wide. Watching our franchisees thrive and grow their businesses is incredibly rewarding. It's not just about making money - it's about creating a community of people who share our values and are passionate about helping children discover their inner calm."

Before I sign off, I want to leave you with one more inspiration story, that of Sam Chetwood, owner of CeCe & Me, a children's shoe-fitting franchise. She says a key driver to franchise her business was "the number of people approaching me for advice about setting up something similar themselves."

Here's her story: "This reinforced my belief in my business concept and the need for a service that supported others, and opened my eyes to the potential I had to help people set up and run a business that works for them and their customers.

Having spent months working hard to put in place the building blocks for a franchise, I arranged my first face-to-face meeting with a potential franchisee. All went very well. She responded positively as I explained how I saw things working, how we would work together and what I could offer. When we parted, she was full of enthusiasm and seemed keen to move forward.

The next day I sent a follow-up email with a summary of what we'd discussed, to which she responded with a couple of questions, I replied and then it all went quiet. Now, I completely understand the decision to start a business is not a quick or easy one, so I didn't expect a quick reply. When she replied a few weeks later to say she'd discussed it in detail with her family and decided not to take it any further, I was disappointed, but the crushing blow was they'd come to the conclusion my business was not franchisable.

I could have crumbled at this point and thrown the towel in. Fortunately, for me and my current and future franchisees, I'm quite stubborn and it just made me even more determined to make the franchise a success. Everything is a learning opportunity and this is what this experience taught me:

- When you're talking to a potential franchisee, they will rarely be making the decision about whether to start their own business by themselves. You are not the only one influencing their decision, so offer to speak to anyone else involved to help address any concerns they have.

- Keep the channels of communication open, this way you can nip any doubts in the bud, before they build into something insurmountable.
- Don't assume everyone already understands the benefits of a franchise and how it works. Make this very clear.
- Starting a business is not for everyone. If someone drops out, even if you think they seemed ideal, it probably wasn't right for them. In most cases, if someone decides not to proceed, it's more about them than it is about you.

You will encounter lots of different personalities and approaches to working, be as sure as you can be that you will be able to work well with a potential franchisee and they will reflect your brand values before you sign on the dotted line!"

This brings us to the end of the book and my six piece jigsaw puzzle to successfully selling franchises. Let's recap those six points one more time:

1. The foundations
2. Franchisee recruitment essentials

3. Discovery Days
4. How to close a franchise sale
5. Franchisor sales mindset
6. Onboarding new franchisees

The power is now in your hands to implement this system and make it yours.

My final thoughts are a bit personal. You need to take care of you. As a franchisor, many other people lay their problems at your door. It is important that you protect your "you" time, take care of your mental health, and spend time with those who love you and lift you higher.

Franchisors are a particular breed of entrepreneur. We strive to be the best we can be and grow our brands with a passion that is rarely seen anywhere else. Don't forget that without you, there is no franchise, so put your oxygen mask on first, always.

ACKNOWLEDGMENTS

Writing this book on the secrets of successfully selling franchises has been a remarkable journey, and I couldn't have accomplished it without the invaluable support and contributions of so many amazing people. I want to take a moment to express my heartfelt gratitude to all those who have made it possible.

First and foremost, a massive thank you to my fabulous husband and awesome children for their unwavering encouragement, patience, and understanding throughout the entire writing process. Your love and support have been my anchor during this incredible journey.

To my dedicated team of professionals who have shared their expertise and insights, thank you for your exceptional commitment to the world of franchising. Your passion for helping entrepreneurs and businesses thrive is truly inspiring.

I'm profoundly grateful to the countless franchisors, franchisees, and industry experts I've had the privilege of working with and learning from over the years. Your stories, experiences, and willingness to share your wisdom have enriched this book immeasurably.

I want to express my gratitude to my mentors and colleagues who have guided me on my journey as a franchise expert. Your wisdom and mentorship have been instrumental in shaping my career and the insights shared in these pages.

I'm indebted to my editor, Victoria Brock, whose keen eye and constructive feedback have transformed this manuscript into a polished and insightful resource.

Last but certainly not least, I extend my thanks to you, the readers, who have entrusted me with your time and attention. It is my hope that this book will provide you with the knowledge and inspiration you need to navigate the complex world of franchising successfully.

To everyone who has played a part in bringing this book to fruition, your support has been the driving force behind its creation. Thank you for your contributions, dedication, and belief in this project.

With love,

Jo Middleton

PRAISE FOR JO

"I have found Jo's coaching to be an invaluable resource for the growth and success of my franchise. Jo's wealth of experience and information has been an incredible asset to us, and I cannot overstate how much we have benefited from her insights and guidance.

One of the most useful aspects of Jo's coaching has been her franchising webinars. These sessions are packed with practical information and advice that we have been able to implement immediately. Jo has a deep understanding of the challenges and opportunities facing franchises like ours, and she has been able to provide us with actionable strategies to help us succeed.

Overall, Jo's coaching has had a significantly positive impact on both me and my franchise. Her guidance and support have helped me to navigate the challenges of running a franchise and grow my business in a sustainable and effective way. I am incredibly grateful for the opportunity to work with Jo, and I would highly recommend her coaching to any other franchisors looking to take their business to the next level."

— Karen Gibb, Mind Marvels

"Working with Jo has been a great experience for me as a franchisor. Through her membership program, I have been provided with lots of resources and training that have proven to be invaluable to every aspect of my franchise recruitment process.

One of the areas that Jo has helped me with is my sales funnel. By working with Jo, I have been able to identify areas where my business could be more efficient and streamlined. With the training available, I have been able to create a sales process that is more effective and is driving better results for my franchise.

Another area where Jo has been an enormous help is in planning my discovery event. Jo helped me plan the event and has been available to answer any questions that I have had, Jo even reviewed my presentation and provided me with feedback and advice. Thanks to Jo's guidance, I was able to put on a successful event that generated significant interest in my franchise opportunity.

One of the things that I appreciate most about working with Jo is her unwavering support and encouragement. She truly is one of the biggest cheerleaders for you and your business. Her genuine desire to see me succeed as a franchisor has been incredibly motivating and has kept me going through the challenges that come with growing a franchise.

Jo has a deep understanding of the franchising industry. She has a wealth of knowledge and expertise that she is more than willing to share with her members."

—Julie Barber, TechyTots Ltd

"The most useful thing about Jo's coaching is that it maintains my focus and attention on the franchise side of my business and the results that have come from that consistency have been amazing. Within the first three months of working with Jo, I had held my first Discovery Day and signed two new franchisees – which was more progress than I had made in the previous two years of my franchising journey!

Jo has a great wealth of knowledge and fantastic network of connections and she is extremely generous with offering up her ideas and suggestions where she feels that they could help you which has been priceless."

— Sarah Mollison, CYCLEme TOTS

"I have only been part of the membership for a short time but really like how approachable and knowledgeable Jo is. I feel I am able to ask any questions I have and everything is broken down so it is simple to follow. The work-along sessions are useful too, so things are actually completed!"

— Joanne Budden, Leapfrog Sports

"Jo is excellent at advising on many things – legal, marketing, discovery days and so much more, but she also brings in mindset. I hadn't realised the important of mindset for a franchisor before working with Jo. Having a franchisor mindset isn't easy when you've been working away in your business for however long and then have to take a step back to see the bigger picture and the bigger goals. It's a work in progress!"

— Sarah Earis, Brilliant Bricks UK Ltd

“I had been a franchisee for eight years before signing up with Jo's framework in mind, so some elements I already understood well. We agreed to evolve my investment in to a new set-up, whereby she can tailor the time we spend together. I am so excited to have a mentor in Jo. I did a lot of research and she is the best in the business.”

— Sarah Dalton, The Baby Cloud

ABOUT THE AUTHOR

Jo Middleton is the founder of Franchise Business School and is on a mission to make ethical franchising easier and more acceptable in the UK. As a bilingual, multiple award-winning serial entrepreneur, author, franchisor and investor who has been in business since 2000, she has a wealth of information to share.

Jo has franchised her own businesses, provided employment opportunities for many, been quoted in Forbes, appeared in numerous publications and television programmes as well as winning several awards including the New Woman Franchisor EWIF 2018 and Best Franchise Support 2019 at the Approved Franchise Association awards. She has spent over a decade studying the habits of successful entrepreneurs and spent tens of thousands of pounds on business coaching, mentorship, personal and professional development with the world's leading business coaches. Jo is a firm believer that you never stop learning.

Free stuff:

10 Most Common Mistakes Made When Franchising

Middleton's Hierarchy of Franchisee Needs

20 Awesome Ideas to Make More Money Now

franchisebusinessschool.com

info@franchiseebusinessschool.com

facebook.com/growmyfranchise

twitter.com/growmyfranchise

instagram.com/FranchiseBusinessSchool

linkedin.com/in/businessgrowthnerd

Printed in Great Britain
by Amazon

29797663R00129